# THE GRAIL

## RONAN COGHLAN

a guide to the world's most sacred mystery

Typeset by Jonathan Downes,
Cover and Layout by SPiderKaT for CFZ Communications
Using Microsoft Word 2000, Microsoft Publisher 2000, Adobe Photoshop CS.

First published in Great Britain by Fortean Words

**CFZ Publishing Group**
**Myrtle Cottage**
**Woolsery**
**Bideford**
**North Devon**
**EX39 5QR**

**First Published 2012**
© Ronan Coghlan 2012

© CFZ MMXII

## ISBN: 978-1-905723-88-1

*for Finn and Rory*

# FOREWORD

The 'Holy' Grail: 'tis the stuff of legends. Whether it relates to a drinking vessel from the Christian era or a great cauldron from an earlier pre-history, it and its contents have fascinated us from early childhood, and - arguably - from 'time in memorial'. Its physical appearance may be varied, and it may indeed be viewed as 'All things to All men'. Its contents, we are told, have 'magical properties' and yes I believe they do, for I believe it contains the Truth, and - as has been said in recent times - the Truth will indeed set you free. So go now and seek your own Grail and your own Truth, and when asked why, you may answer that "You are on a King's Quest".

Blessings from Stonehenge
King Arthur Pendragon
Battlechieftain
Council of British Druid Orders
2012

# INTR⊕DUCTI⊕N

**W**hat is the Grail? Whom does it serve?"

This is the famous Grail Question on which the whole tale hinges; but most people have quite a vague idea of what the whole myth of the Grail is about or even what the Grail actually is. As many books have appeared on the subject, ranging from the scholarly to the amateur, producing various theories which might well mislead the ordinary reader, the aim of this work is to include ideas from all sides, however absurd some may seem.

The Grail, in fact, seems to have popped out of nowhere in the 12th Century. The poet Chrétien de Troyes, who flourished in that century, produced a work called *Perceval; ou Le Conte de Graal.* The story, as Chrétien unfolds it, has no predecessors that have survived. Yet various scholars do not for a moment think he fabricated the whole tale *ex nihilo.* There are too many characters and motifs that are found in earlier sources for that to be at all likely.

The source of Chrétien's poems is undoubtedly to be found among Celtic myths. During the period of Roman rule in Britain, the Britons converted to Christianity. However, as was often the case, the conversion was only partial. The gods of the pagan Britons were transformed into heroes of yore and the myths surrounding them became transformed into their exploits.

When the Romans withdrew from Britain, the Britons found themselves faced with an enemy in the form of the Anglo-Saxons, who invaded the country and conquered most of it in the 6th Century AD. The unconquered Britons became the ancestors of the Welsh and Cornish. They continued to develop a rich oral and sometimes written literature, dealing with their numerous legends and traditions. A great number of them also migrated to Brittany, where they became the ancestors of today's Breton speakers. The myths of the Welsh and Cornish continued to thrive amongst the Breton minstrels.

These Bretons did not keep the tales they told to themselves. They were only too willing to share their sagas with French poets who made good use of the material. One such was Chrétien de Troyes.

Chrétien's story cannot be traced back to a British original. There are, however, elements in it which are clearly derived from British sources. There are even some that come from Irish sources, as there was considerable Irish occupation of parts of Britain in the latter part of the Roman period. Although the British Celtic element is readily discernable, a secondary element may have been the discussion taking place in the Church at the time about the subject of Transubstantiation - in other words, the question of in what way Jesus Christ was present in the Sacred Host.

Chretien's grail is used as a common noun. He does not use the word *grail* to signify a particular and singular kind of dish. *Grail* was an ordinary word in such southern French languages as Provençal and Catalan. This grail, however, was performing an unusual function. It was part of a procession which can only be described as bizarre. It contained the Sacred Host, but liturgically this procession was inappropriate. It blazed with light. The Sacred Host was used to serve an injured king. It left the hero of the story, Perceval, completely puzzled. Little did he know that the whole Grail Mystery hinged on a question he should have asked but didn't.

We do not know how Chrétien's story would have turned out, as he died before finishing it. Continuators were not slow to continue it. However, in Germany, Wolfram von Eschenbach wrote his own version which was much like Chrétien's, but he threw in various oriental touches and claimed his story was the true version. Moreover, he insisted that the Grail was no vessel but a stone. The person who made what might be termed the Big Addition was one Robert de Boron.

In Robert's case, he took various pieces of information from Christian lore and made them into the story of how the Grail reached Britain in the first place in his poem *Joseph of Arimathea.* Robert's poem has a thoroughly Christian stamp and identifies the Grail with the Cup of the Last Supper. He uses on one occasion the word *chalice* to describe it. This is far more specific than and also rather unlike the vessel described by Chrétien. A further romance, the *Estoire de Saint Graal,* says Joseph actually brought the Grail to Britain. This was to be followed by the tradition that Joseph founded a Christian settlement at Glastonbury and this led legends surrounding that famous monastery to become entangled with Grail stories.

At a more Celtic level, a Welsh writer produced *Peredur*, which, though influenced by Chrétien, also had native British elements, including the startling fact that, instead of a Grail, the procession contained a head. It may be that in the original British tale, the Grail contained a head for some oracular purpose.

The *Queste du Saint-Graal,* written, it is thought, under the influence of the Cistercian Order, gives us what is in many respects the standard Grail Quest story. In this, Perceval is largely replaced by a new hero, Galahad. Galahad is supposed to be a Christ-like figure and he, Perceval and Bors finally attain the Grail. This is the version used by Thomas Malory, which has rendered it so familiar to readers of English.

There were other versions of the Grail quest which are dealt with in the body of this volume.

The story of the Grail Quest is set in the time of King Arthur. If he lived, his likely dates would be between 450-550; but scholars are in disagreement over whether he was a real or a mythical personage.

The adventures of Joseph of Arimathea, on the other hand, would have been set in the First Century AD. Something of a mythos has grown up about Joseph, suggesting he visited Britain on several occasions, even bringing Jesus with him. These ideas and traditions are all dealt with here.

A late idea, first found by the writer John Hardyng (1378-1465), is that the words *San Greal* (Holy Grail) should really be interpreted as *Sang Real* (royal blood). This has led to an idea that has surfaced in modern times to the effect that the Grail represented a bloodline, with the further qualification that this bloodline represented a line of descent from Jesus Christ and Mary Magdalen. This appeared in *The Holy Blood and the Holy Grail* (1982) and was supposedly a secret preserved by a secret society, the Priuré de Sion, one of whose grand masters, Leonardo da Vinci, helpfully left a clue in his painting of *The Last Supper.*

The idea was espoused by Laurence Gardner and also formed the subject of Dan Brown's novel *The Da Vinci Code* (2003) which has led to wide interest today. These suggestions are all explored in this work, as are the persons concerned with their dissemination.

Finally, a reference book like this should contain all theories regarding the Grail, all the important characters in the Grail story and all the authorities on which the story is based. The present work, however, contains an Epilogue in which the author puts forwards his own suggestion regarding the origin of the story. He puts this suggestion forward as hypothesis, not fact, and will listen with attention to alternative ideas.

The story of the Grail is not merely a tale of knightly prowess. Rather, it is a saga of mystery and wonder. This is no doubt what has rendered it a source of fascination to the imaginative and one which, in these materialistic times, makes the goals of modern society - wealth, status, career, possessions - seem merely pallid by comparison.

# ABBREVIATIONS OF SOURCE WORKS USED IN THE TEXT

**Albrecht:** Albrecht, *Jungerer Titurel*
**Chrétien:** Chrétien de Troyes
*Estoire:* Estoire de Saint-Graal
**Geoffrey:** Geoffrey of Monmouth
**Malory:** T. Malory *Le Morte d'Arthur*
*Perlesvaus: Perlesvaus* also called *High History of the Holy Grail*
*Queste:* Queste del Saint Graal
**Robert:** Robert de Boron *Joseph d'Arimathie*
**Wolfram:** Wolfram von Eschenbach

The Continuations of Chrétien de Troyes are merely called First Continuation, Second Continuation, Third Continuation and Fourth Continuation

*The following are the titles of works in the* Mabinogion. The *Mabinogion* is a collection of medieval Welsh tales.

*Branwen*
*Culhwch ac Olwen*
*Peredur*

Asterisks are appended to words in articles to show they have articles of their own. This system, however, is not applied to the names of works or sources.

The Holy Grail

# A

**ACCOKEEK**  A town (population 7300) in Maryland.  A local legend says that  Captain John Smith sailed up the Potomac in about 1606 and was accompanied by a priest who was said to have somehow obtained the Grail*.  He hid it somewhere in the area, but its location is unknown.

A variant of this legend says that Smith taught local Indians "the Grail".  Perhaps this means he taught them its history.

**ACHMARDI**  Wolfram tells us that the Grail*, which he conceives as a stone, was brought in on a tissue of this substance.  It is in fact emerald, from Arabic *az-zumurud.*

**ACORANT**  A knight who went on the Grail* Quest, but was killed in the process by one Apiant of the Narrow Mountain.

**ADAN**  Son of Joseph of Arimathea* in *Sone de Nausay.*

**AESOP'S BED**  A rock near Talland in Cornwall.  H.A. Lewis suggests that Aesop was a corruption of *Joseph*, supporting the legend that Joseph of Arimathea* visited Cornwall.

**AKASHIC RECORDS**  A term coined by Madame Blavatsky[1] from Sanskrit *akasha*, 'ether'.  She contended that in the ether was a record of everything that has happened and that this could be accessed.  One or two Grail* researchers have tried to employ this method.  The only trouble is, if this record actually exists, there seems to be no way of distinguishing it from the products of one's imagination.

---

1. Helena Petrovna Blavatsky (Russian: Еле́на Петро́вна Блава́тская, Ukrainian: Олена Петрівна Блаватська), (born as Helena von Hahn (Russian: Елена Петровна Ган, Ukrainian: Олена Петрівна Ган); 12 August [O.S. 31 July] 1831 – 8 May 1891) was a theosophist, writer and traveler. While Blavatsky claims that she went around the world three times, between 1848 and 1875, her stories are often contradictory and some scholars are skeptical about the veracity of her claims. In 1875 Blavatsky, together with Colonel H. S. Olcott, established the Theosophical Society. One of the main purposes of this Society was "to form a nucleus of the Universal Brotherhood of Humanity, without distinction of race, creed, sex, caste or color". Blavatsky discussed the major themes of Theosophy in several works, including The Secret Doctrine, Isis Unveiled, The Key to Theosophy, and The Voice of the Silence. (From Wikipedia, the free encyclopedia)

**ALAN**

**1.** The son of Bron* and Enygeus*, we are told in the *Estoire* that he converted King Alphasen to Christianity, but later wounded him in the thigh for sleeping in the Grail Castle* of Corbenic*. He had chosen to be celibate and was placed in charge of his brothers and sisters. In the *Didot-Perceval* he was Perceval's* father, the author not having realised that many generations separated the two.

R.S. Loomis has suggested that he may be in origin *Arawn*, an otherworldly king in Welsh mythology.

**2.** In some sources, the name of Perceval's brother.

**3.** A knight who went on the Grail* Quest, called Alan of the Meadows.

*If the name is taken from Celtic mythology, rather than being the medieval Scottish or Breton name, there may be some connection with the name of the Gaulish god* Alaunus. Cf. *also Welsh* alaw, *'harmony'.* The Alans, a barbarian tribe, became powerful in Brittany where *Alan* as a consequence became a popular name and from there the name Alan may have found its way into the Grail story.

**ALAWIS** A Muslim sect with unusual beliefs found in Syria and other parts of the Levant as shown in this map, which like the image of a typical Alawi man in the years before WW2 appears courtesy of Wikimedia Commons.

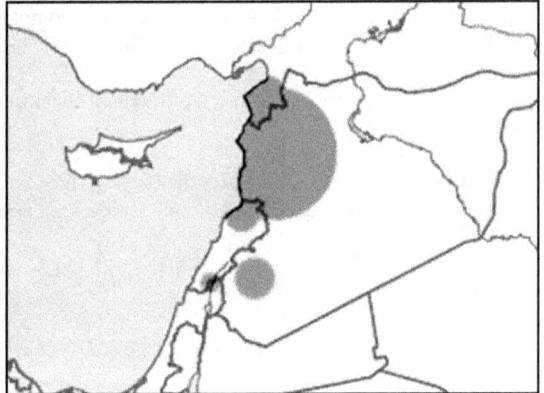

It has been suggested the Alawi are of Hittite descent, but this is uncertain. Their religious beliefs are said to incorporate Christian, pagan and gnostic elements. Their doctrines were kept highly secret, known only to a few even amongst the Alawis themselves.

W.N. Birks[1], when talking to one of the more expert of their number was told that the Grail* (as he explained it to his informant) represented a secret doctrine that Jesus* taught to John the Apostle. Heavenly wine can be taken if the imbiber can find an appropriate vessel. They hold that the vessel is the person himself, if he can hold the divine essence. Jesus did this and is a living Grail. He held the Godhead to the extent a man can hold the Godhead. This, at least, is the belief amongst the Ghaibiya group.

Birks suggests a Crusader may have heard this doctrine and brought it back to France, where it could have gone into the formation of the Grail saga.

**ALBRECHT** The author of the Grail* poem *Der Jungerer Titurel* (13th Century). It expands on Wolfram and was once thought to have been written by Wolfram himself. Subsequently, the author was misidentified as Albrecht von Scharfenberg, but is now held to be a different Albrecht.

---

1. Co-author of *The Treasure of Montsegur: Study of the Cathar Heresy and the Nature of the Cathar Secret* (1987). This book should not be confused with a novel called *The Treasure of Montsegur* (2003) by Sophy Burnham.

---

**ALCHEMY**  One of the purposes of alchemy was to find the Philosopher's Stone to make man a spiritual being, paralleling the transformation of Galahad* when he looked into the Grail*.  The use of a stone for

the Grail by Wolfram may indicate an alchemical influence in his work.

The elements needed to produce the Philosopher's Stone were placed in a vessel called an alembic, which could represent a Grail.

Another purpose of alchemy was to transmute base metals into gold, but according to Paracelsus (1493-1541), this was not gold commonly so called, perhaps indicating a spiritual enlightenment.

The rather unflattering image reproduced here is a 17th Century engraving of Paracelsus based on the slightly less wrinkled image in an engraving by Wenceslaus Hollar (1607-1677)

**ALIBEL**  A knight who went on the Grail* Quest.

**ALIEN-GRAIL INTERACTION**  It is contended on the website www.montalk.net that the Grail* guardians of Wolfram are aliens who interbred with humans, adding to the DNA of both parents so the offspring may resemble both.  The website regards the Grail as a supernatural object brought to the earth from an Otherworld*.  The Ark of the Covenant*, they say, may have contained it.

**ALISTANS**  A knight who went on the Grail* Quest.

**ALTROMH TIGH DÁ MEDAR**  A.G. van Hamel[1] searched for a Celtic story that had the same sort of components that the Grail* history had, without its being the Grail story itself.  He found it in this story in the Book of Fermoy (Irish).  It tells the story of Eithne, who would only drink the milk from the Dun Cow or the Speckled Cow.  Manannán (the Irish sea-god, now regarded as a fairy being) realised this was because she was a Christian.  Just like the Grail story, this tale mixes Christian and pagan elements.  Although it is not ancestral to the Grail story, it shows that a mixture of such elements was not foreign to the Celtic mentality.

**ALYUBA**  The website www.biblesearchers.com claims that this was the name of the wife of Joseph of Arimathea*.  The present writer has no knowledge of how they acquired such information.

**AMANGONS**  The *Elucidation* tells us that the court of the Fisher King* vanished when King Amangons and his followers violated the well maidens whose duty it was to feed travellers.  The well maidens and their descendants ended by wandering about, looking for the Rich Fisher*.  The well maidens are obviously those spirits who supplied nourishment for the country.  Without their exercising their office as tutelary spirits, the country would become unproductive.  King Amangons should not be confused with the King of Greenland who bore the same name elsewhere in Arthurian legend, though perhaps originally both were identical.

**AMAGUSA SHIRO**  When the Japanese Government outlawed Christianity, Amagusa Shiro, then aged 16, led a Christian rebellion.  His flag displayed the Grail* with the Host and the letters INRI.  Some of his followers spread it about that he was the Second Coming of Christ.  His army of 37,000 was overwhelmed

---

1. Anton Gerard van Hamel (5 July 1886, Hilversum - 23 November 1945, Utrecht)) was a Dutch scholar, best known for his contributions to Celtic and Germanic studies, especially those relating to literature, linguistics, philology and mythology. He is not to be confused with his uncle, Anton Gerard van Hamel (1842-1907), who was a theologian, professor of French and editor of De Gids. (From Wikipedia, the free encyclopedia)

by government forces numbering 120,000 in 1637 and he died on the battlefield. The rebellion was known as the Shimaban Rebellion. He was also known as Amakusa Shirō Tokisada

**AMBELAIN, ROBERT** (1907-1997) This French author had written a book saying Jesus* had a concubine. It has been asserted that this gave the BBC team of Baigent, Lincoln* and Leigh the idea to trace the Merovingians* to a marriage of Jesus* and Mary Magdalene*., making the Bloodline* of their descendants the Grail*. Ambelain had apparently been introduced to Lincoln by Pierre Plantard*.

**AMINADAB** Son of Joshua*, a Grail King*. According to Laurence Gardner, he married Eurgen, daughter of King Lucius*.

**AMPFLISE** A Grail* Maiden in Wolfram.

**ANASCOR** A companion of Joseph of Arimathea* in the *Estoire*.

**ANCIENT TECHNOLOGY** Patricia and Lionel Fanthorpe suggest, merely as a possibility, that the Grail* was an object made by extraterrestrials or an ancient but forgotten technology on earth. As Lionel Fanthorpe was once an astonishingly prolific science fiction writer, this is not surprising.

**ANFORTAS** This is the name of the Grail King* in Wolfram. His castle was called Munsalvaesche*. He had been wounde4d for taking part in a tournament in service to a lady. His name may be derived from Latin *infirmitas* or Old French *enfertez,* 'infirmity'. The derivation given by L. Gardner from *in fortis* is inaccurate. Anfortas was Perceval's* maternal uncle, the brother of Herzeloyde*. Gardner, in arguing for his place in the Bloodline*, says he was also called Boaz. Perceval healed him by asking the Grail Question*. In Wagner, he is named *Amfortas.*

**ANNA** A number of Welsh pedigrees go back to Anna, cousin of the Virgin Mary. She is said to have been either the wife or daughter of Beli As Beli was a god, Anna was presumably one too, having been Christianised in medieval times. She is perhaps a Welsh version of the Irish mother goddess Anu. This goddess is thought identical with the British goddess Dôn.

Related to her appearance in early pedigrees may be the Breton legend of St Anne, mother of the Virgin Mary. The name of the Virgin's mother is not supplied in the Bible, but is given as Anne in the apocryphal *Protevangelium of James* and may be based on a genuine tradition. Breton legend made her a Breton. It said she was mistreated by her husband who cast her out when he discovered she was expecting the Virgin, but was taken to Israel, where she gave birth. She later returned to Brittany (the angel again providing transport) where Jesus as an adult visited her. While there, he drove his staff into the ground and a fountain sprang up.

However, L. Gardner used her in his Bloodline* argument. He says Joseph of Arimathea* married her and they had a daughter also called Anna who was identical with Enygeus*. The second Anna married Bran/Bron*; Beli was their son and Penardun their daughter.

The idea of Beli's being the son of Anna may have come from J. Lewis *History of Great Britain* (1729), where he said Beli was the son of An, daughter of Einya, brother of St Elizabeth, the mother of John the Baptist.

Penardun Is mentioned in Welsh literature (*Branwen*) as the mother rather than the daughter of Bran. The website Missouri-mule.com cites a remark that Anna may have been descended from Joseph's first wife, Escha.

**ANNUNAKI** The gods of Sumer and Akkad. The Sumerian civilization, which started in southern Iraq perhaps 5000 years ago, was succeeded by the Akkadian. It has been suggested by several peripheral archaeological figures, notably Zecharia Sitchin, that the Annunaki were in fact extraterrestrials or ultraterrestrials and the stories about them are basically historical. Nonetheless, if one reads the original texts about them, such as the Babylonian *Enuma Elish*, they seem to reflect pure mythology more than anything else.

Laurence Gardner claims they were historical persons of a race antedating humanity. They retained their youth by drinking their menstrual blood, which they called Star Fire. Menstrual blood can be of a purplish hue with blobs shaped like pineapple chunks in it, hardly of enticing appearance, but this did not deter the Annunaki. They interbred with humans and Cain* was the son of one of their number by Eve and he was the first king of the Grail* bloodline. Members of the Bloodline continued to maintain their youth by imbibing menstrual blood. The Annunaki seem to have done a disappearing act, which Gardner dates at BC 1960, and, their menstrual blood gone, the only way for the members of the Bloodline to defer to stay youthful was to eat ground gold.

The menstrual blood was supposed to have produced extra melatonin, which resulted in the Annunaki's longevity and the longevity of humans to whom they gave it. There is in fact not a shred of evidence that melatonin, or ground gold for that matter, prolongs life. This ground gold was, Gardner claims, the *lapis exilis* of Wolfram.

**ANNWFN** (Modern Welsh *Annwn*; from Celtic **anduluos*, 'underworld') The otherworld to which Arthur and his men ventured in the obscure early poem *Preiddeu Annwfn*. This seems to have been a Celtic paradise and had to be reached by ship, perhaps indicating it lay across the Western Ocean. That it was regarded as a paradisal realm may be inferred from the Breton word *Annaon* (Heaven). As it was probably the dwelling place of the pagan gods, in Christian times it came to be seen as a kind of infernal realm, where Gwyn ab Nudd* had been put in charge of the demons. It contained a cauldron* which may have been a prototype of the Grail*. There can be little doubt that this is the same otherworld as Avalon*. Indeed, in a Welsh version of Giraldus, Avalon is translated as Annwfyn.

The idea of otherworlds* in the sense of coexisting universes is now beginning to appeal to some modern physicists.

**ANTIOCH CHALICE** An object discovered in 1910, which , it was suggested, was the Grail*. Its style is 6th Century. It is in fact now thought to be a lamp. It is currently in the Metropolitan Museum of Art, New York.

Another Antioch Chalice was also thought to be possibly the Grail, but this was queried in *Antiquity* (1935).

**APPRENTICE PILLAR** A pillar in Rosslyn* Chapel. According to a legend, which cannot be traced before the 18th Century, the sculptor went away to see the original pillar on which the structure was to be based. On returning, he found his apprentice had already completed the project, so he killed him in jealousy.

The pillar is supposed to contain a cavity in which the Grail* reposes. It has been contended that, if such a hole existed, the weakness of the pillar would cause the roof to fall in. A scan of the Pillar revealed neither the Grail or anything else within it. K. Laidler, who thinks the Grail is the embalmed head* of Christ, thinks it is buried beneath the Pillar.

**ARCULF**  A Frankish pilgrim of the 7th Century who claimed to have touched the cup of the Last Supper near Jerusalem.

**ARDAGH CHALICE**  This artefact has been identified by M. Cottrell with the Holy Grail*.  It is a silver cup with gilt wire, glass and enamel decorations.  It has two handles and is 6" high.  Dated by archaeologists to the 8th Century, it is now in the National Museum of Ireland.  It was discovered in 1868 in County Limerick.

**Ardagh Chalice (Kglavin/Wikipedia)**

Cottrell has the idea that the sun affects fertility (a fact, he says, known to the Maya) and has a magnetic reversal every 1,366,040 days.  Cottrell maintains that the early Celts knew of this.  The super-science of the sun is encoded in the artefact, probably on Jesus' instructions.  Cottrell asserts Jesus taught this super-science.

Cottrell argues the only real reason for the official dating of the chalice is the carving of the apostles' names in insular majuscule script, but he avers these carvings could be later than the rest of the chalice.  He suggests that Arthur* discovered the Tara Brooch* and, decoding it, found out that the Ardagh Chalice was the Grail. Both were later taken to Ireland to avoid plundering enemies.

His reasons for identifying the chalice with the Grail are several. These include esoteric information on the 365 day year and the 366 day leap year, which he is sure is to be found on the vessel. He says a missing bowl rim stud amongst those with the apostles' names indicates the future betrayal by Judas. He says the subconical suds make it possible to take part in a virtual crucifixion.

**ARGUS** Galahad's* brother in the Welsh *Y Sant Greal.* The brother of the Grail* hero seems peculiar to this work.

**ARK OF THE COVENANT** It was probably only a matter of time, given the publicity attendant on the mystery of the Ark (*aron*) of the Covenant, that the question of whether it was the Grail* would arise. According to the Bible, the Ark was built as the Hebrews were journeying from Egypt to the Promised Land. It contained the tablets of the Ten Commandments. It was made of acacia wood, covered with gold inside and out. On top was the mercy seat (*kapporet*). Two cherubim at either end of the mercy-seat had their wings extended over it. It had two rings of gold on each side attached to its feet. Through these wooden poles, covered with gold, were placed and they could not be removed.

The Ark seems to have been rather dangerous, killing people who approached it even if they had done nothing wrong. It has been suggested it was some kind of weapon and brought down the walls of Jericho. When it was placed in the Temple, it was kept in a dark room and the high priest went in there, perhaps timorously, only once a year. When Solomon's Temple was destroyed (BC 587), the Ark may have been destroyed with it. A letter in the Second Book of Maccabees supposedly written by the prophet Jeremiah says the Ark was hidden in a cave on Mount Nebo. In the Talmud it is said Josiah hid it in a place prepared by King Solomon in case the Temple were attacked.

Henrietta Bernstein, however, is of the opinion that it contained the Emerald Tablet of Hermes Trismegistus[1] and says that the Ark, the teachings of Christ and the tableware of the Last Supper were all part of the Grail*. They were brought to Glastonbury*. Arthur* was their guardian. Merlin's* schools disseminated them amongst the heads of nations.

Graham Hancock postulated that the Ark and the Grail were identical as far as Wolfram was concerned. He suggested the Templars* were in Ethiopia for a time and had seen it there. The Ethiopian Church keeps in its churches *tabotat*, wooden or stone tablets, which are referred to as arks. The original Ark of the Covenant is supposed by the Ethiopians to be in the cathedral at Axum. It is said by some that it is merely a slab, one of the tablets of Moses, not a container. It is kept in a secretive area of the cathedral. The belief amongst the Ethiopians is that Solomon, King of Israel, had an intrigue with the Queen of Sheba, who was called Makeda. When she returned to her kingdom, she gave birth to a son, Menelik, who eventually returned to Israel, where his followers stole the Ark when they made their way home. The Ethiopian book relating the story, the *Kebra Nagast,* is of uncertain date. The Queen of Sheba is thought by some to have been a ruler of the Sabaeans, an Arabian people. However, there was a place called Saba in Ethiopia in pre-Axumite times. H. Adolf had already said in 1947 that Wolfram had heard of the *tabot* and used it for his Grail. In Abu-Salih's *Chronicle* (13th Century), it is said that the Ark was carried four times a year by descendants of David's family, whose skin was white and red and who had blond hair.

Hancock feels these people may have been Templars* and the 16th Century Portuguese ambassador Alvarez heard that the famous rock hewn churches of the Emperor Lalibela, who lived in medieval times, had been constructed by white men. All this would indicate a white population in Ethiopia in the 13th Century who might have brought back tales of the Ark with its sacred tablet to Europe, thereby contributing to the Grail mythos.

In fact, the question of colouration may be due to a misunderstanding. The Ethiopians referred to themselves as 'red' to distinguish them from even blacker races.

**ARK OF THE GRAIL** The receptacle in which the Grail* was kept on its way to Britain in the *Estoire.* On one occasion when Josephes* opened it, he beheld a man in red and five six-winged angels. He saw Christ on the cross and his blood running into the Grail*. Joseph* looked in and saw an altar caparisoned with white cloths, under which lay samite* covering three nails, a Lance* head and a dish. In the centre was a vessel of gold, silver and jewels. Seven angels emerged carrying water, a watering pot, gold basins, towels and gold censers. An eighth angel came out carrying a holy dish and a ninth with a head of

---

1. Hermes Trismegistus (Greek: Ἑρμῆς ὁ Τρισμέγιστος, "thrice-greatest Hermes"; Latin: Mercurius ter Maximus) is the eponymous author of the Hermetic Corpus, a sacred text belonging to the genre of divine revelation.

He may be a representation of the syncretic combination of the Greek god Hermes and the Egyptian god Thoth. In Hellenistic Egypt, the Greeks recognised the congruence of their god Hermes with the Egyptian god Thoth. Subsequently the two gods were worshipped as one in what had been the Temple of Thoth in Khemnu, which the Greeks called Hermopolis. Both Thoth and Hermes were gods of writing and of magic in their respective cultures. Thus, the Greek god of interpretive communication was combined with the Egyptian god of wisdom as a patron of astrology and alchemy. (Adapted from Wikipedia)

beauty that exceeded anything seen before. The tenth angel carried a sword, then came three more with tapers and finally came Christ, who made Josephes a bishop.

The idea for an Ark of the Grail was probably inspired by the Ark of the Covenant*.

**ARTHUR** The story of the Grail* quest is always placed in the reign of King Arthur. The question that most people ask is whether this monarch ever really existed and this we cannot say with certainty. According to legend, after the Romans had withdrawn from Britain, he led resistance against invading Angles, Saxons, Scots and Picts.

J. Morris favoured the existence of an historical Arthur whose reign commenced in the 470s. D. Dumville, on the other hand, makes him a purely legendary character, saying no evidence can be adduced in favour of his historicity. This does not mean, as some have said, that Dumville disproved the existence of Arthur.T. Green has voiced the opinion that he was really a god and that Nennius (9th Century; probably not the real name of the author) in his *Historia Brittonum* was the first to write of his career in historical terms; before that, he had merely been associated with timeless supernatural adventures. It might be mentioned that there was a Gaulish god called Artaio, an inscription to whom was found in the village of Beaucroissant (Isère). This village was once called Artay, while a village of the same name is to be found near Grenoble.

Whether Arthur was historical or not, there was in the 5th Century an "Arthur-shaped gap" in which the Anglo-Saxon invaders of Britain were contained and peace reigned. This was after the Battle of Mount Badon, which the near-contemporary writer Gildas mentions. Gildas, however, was not an historian *per se* and does not mention Arthur. Nennius asserts Badon was Arthur's final victory in his cycle of twelve battles.

The *Annales Cambriae* says there were 21 years between Badon and Arthur's demise. There is of course the famous legend that Arthur never died, but was taken to the Isle of Avalon* to recuperate and will one day return. A variant of this is that Arthur and his men are sleeping in some cave and will one day come back.

In *Perlevaus* it would seem that Arthur is, to some extent an enfeebled king. He planned to go to the Chapel of St Austin to pray about the matter, but, before he did so, his page Chaus woke up to find a knife sticking into him. Dying, he told Arthur he had dreamt of going into the forest where he found a chapel, containing a dead knight surrounded by candlesticks. He removed one candlestick to prove his adventure, but, on the way home, he had encountered a giant who demanded he hand it over. When he refused, the giant struck him and he awoke to find himself fatally wounded.

Arthur observed a Mass at the chapel and, on his way back, a voice told him that the world was in a sorry state and that he should do something about it. As a result, he proclaimed the Grail Quest at Penzance. Three damsels rode into the hall. One told Arthur that, as a result of Perceval's* failure to ask the Grail Question*, she had lost her hair. One brought a hound, destined to greet whomsoever achieved the Grail joyfully and the shield of Joseph of Arimathea*; and one who wore a star, which she held, while on the other hand she had a whip with which she urged on the horses of the other damsels. Joseph's shield was to hang upon the wall, to be awarded to the achiever of the Grail.

Time passed and one evening Arthur saw a ship steered by a venerable man. Perceval was aboard. He had succeeded in his quest, so he was awarded shield and hound and then returned to the Grail. Arthur later visited him and himself saw the Grail.

Arthur features in what may be a prototype of the Grail Quest. The poem is narrated by Taliesin*, who is himself one of the characters. It is a Welsh work called *Preideu Annwfn* (modern *Preiddeu Annwn**).It tells how Arthur and a band of followers set out for *Annwfn*, the otherworld. This seems to have been seen as a kind of co-existing universe, of the kind such physicists as Michio Kaku speak of today. It tells of the cauldron* of the ruler (*pen*) of that place, blue-edged with pearl, which would not boil the food of a coward. Of the expedition, only seven of the adventurers returned. However, what is generally regarded as a somewhat euhemerised versiion of this tale takes place in the Welsh romance of *Culhwch ac Olwen*.

Here Culhwch, Arthur's cousin, is assigned a number of tasks by a giant, so he may win the hand of Olwen, his daughter. Arthur and his men agree to help Culhwch.. One of the tasks is to obtain the caul-dron of Diwrnach*, who lives in Ireland, a rationalisation of the Otherworld. They set off in Arthur's ship, *Prydwen*. Bedwyr (Bedivere*) grasped the cauldron and placed it on the back of Arthur's servant Hygwydd, while Arthur's follower Llenleog, himself an Irishman, laid into and slew Diwrnach's follow-ers with the sword Caledfwlch (=Excalibur). They took the cauldron back to Dyfed.

**ARTHUR OF LITTLE BRITAIN** This character is the hero of a non-Arthurian romance of the same name, written in the 14th Century. The little Britain concerned is Brittany. Although the hero is distinct from King Arthur*, R.S. Loomis thinks they were once identical. He entered a castle and underwent there adventures such as those undergone by others in the Arthurian Grail Castle*. It might be the case that the tale was originally based on one of Arthur himself visiting the Grail Castle*.

**ARTHUR THE LESS** Natural son of Arthur*, he went on the Grail* Quest and was present when Galahad* obtained the Grail.

**ARTHURIAN GRAIL** S.L.I. Pettit has suggested that the Grail* was made in the lifetime of Arthur*,

who used it as a status symbol, perhaps supposedly endowed with miraculous powers. He may even have devised a Grail ritual inspired by the rituals of Mithras[1] on the Continent. This would have heartened his own followers and perhaps affrighted his enemies.

**ARTHUR'S SEAT** Mountain in Edinburgh, allegedly called after King Arthur*. The Grail* is said to have been concealed in a cave at its base.

**ARVIRAGUS** Little is known of this Briton, except that he appears to have been in conflict with Rome during the reign of Domitian (81-96 AD). This is the only information we have for certain about this personage. It is not impossible, as some have contended, that Arviragus was a title rather than a personal name.

---

1. The Mithraic Mysteries was a mystery religion practised in the Roman Empire from about the 1st to 4th centuries AD. The name of the Persian god Mithra, adapted into Greek as Mithras, was linked to a new and distinctive imagery. Romans also called the religion Mysteries of Mithras or Mysteries of the Persians; modern historians refer to it as Mithraism, or sometimes Roman Mithraism. The mysteries were popular in the Roman military.

Worshippers of Mithras had a complex system of seven grades of initiation, with ritual meals. Initiates called themselves syndexioi, those "united by the handshake". They met in underground temples (called a mithraeum), which survive in large numbers. The cult appears to have had its epicentre in Rome. (From Wikipedia, the free encyclopedia)

Geoffrey says he was king of Britain and married Genuissa, daughter of the Emperor Claudius. He later clashed with Vespasian (reigned 69-79 AD), but peace was established and he continued as king. This is all balderdash. Britain (except Scotland) was conquered by the Romans in Claudius' time.

In the Welsh version of Geoffrey entitled *Brut y Brenhinedd* we find his name cymrified as *Gweirydd*. In some Welsh traditions we find the adjective *adairweinidog* 'bird servants' applied to him. This presumably means he had avian underlings.

Arviragus is supposed to have given Joseph of Arimathea* leave to preach in Britain and twelve hides of land around Glastonbury. A hide is normally 120 acres, but in Glastonbury it was 160 acres. The first person to mention this seems to be John of Tinmouth (14th Century). It is also stated by John Hardying (15th Century). Arviragus refused baptism from Joseph according to Geoffrey, but Hardyng claims he accepted it. Gardner says he was king of Siluria, a region in southern Wales.

**ASHBURY CAMP** An earthwork in Cornwall. It may have been identified with the Grail Castle*, as it was known in the 12th Century as Caer Beli, if we assume Pelleas* is a development of Beli (a Celtic god). It was regarded in local folklore as a fairy castle.

**AVALON** This seems to be a kind of Celtic paradise and may well be identical with Annwfn* or a portion of it.

Geoffrey says in *Historia Regum Brittaniae* that Arthur was taken there to be healed. In his other work, the *Vita Merlini*, he calls it *insula pomorum*, Isle of Apples. Giraldus Cambrensis, the first to identify Avalon with Glastonbury* in writing, seems uncertain whether it derived its name from apples or from a king named Avallo. Guillaume de Rennes pictured it as an Elysium ruled by a king named Avallo. The interpolated version of William of Malmesbury says it may have been called after an Avalloc who lived there with his daughters. Ralph of Coggeshall claims the apples were the source of the name. It was also known in French literature in the 12th Century, where it was associated with gold. We do not have to look far in dealing with otherworlds to identify the god Afallach with Avallo/Avalloc. Whether his name is connected with apples or not seems to be a matter of dispute. The similarity of the words may have led to a connection that did not originally exist. (Welsh *afal*, Celtic *\*aballo*). An interesting feature is that the delights of Avalon seem to be natural, not man-made.

Geoffrey says that Morgan* brought Arthur there to be healed. He says she dwelt there with her eight sisters. These bear a resemblance to the Nine Maidens* who attended the Cauldron* that we suspect could have been a prototype of the Grail* in the poem *Preiddeu Annwfn\**.

The identification of Glastonbury with Avalon may have been due to the supposed discovery of Arthur's remains there; but it may always have been regarded as a gateway to the otherworld, the actual portal being on the Tor. One might add that Avalon has been identified by some with locations other than Glastonbury - the isle of Aval off the coast of Brittany, the Isle of Man, the modern Burgh by Sands (Cumbria), which was called Aballava in Roman times, and the island of Bardsey, one of the places where Merlin is said to lie buried. The term 'Vale of Avalon' was used for a location near Tintagel in Cornwall, where Arthur was supposedly born. H. Jenner has suggested it was Bosava in Cornwall. P. Coppens suggests Anglesea (Welsh *Môn*). Whitehead favours the Isle of Wight. R. Castleden considers Whithorn (Galloway).

Avalon is probably identical with Amilion and Oléron, magical places mentioned in minor Arthurian romances. It may also be identical with the kingdom of Escavalon, ruled by Perceval's uncle Elinant, in *Perlesvaus*.

# B

**BAGARIM** One of the knights who went on the Grail* Quest.

**BAGDEMAGUS** King of Gorre, he played a minor part in the Grail* Quest. The present writer suspects Gorre is another name for Glastonbury*. The chief city of Gorre was Gorrun.

**BALIN** An Arthurian knight from Northumberland, known as the Knight of the Two Swords. He had a brother called Balan and, one assumes, unimaginative parents when it came to names. He killed an evil knight called Garlon, who had the power of invisibility. Garlon's brother Pellam* tried to kill Balin, but Balin pierced him with the Grail Lance*. In this way, Pellam became the Maimed King. Another tale set some time earlier tells how Brulan killed Lambor*, the Grail King*. Brulan and Balin are fairly clearly identical. Balin and his brother, not recognising each other in their armour, eventually killed each other.

**BAMBERG GREENSTONE** A stone in Bamberg Diocesan Museum which, it has been suggested, inspired Wolfram with his idea to have the Grail* as a stone.

**BANYERS** One of the knights who went on the Grail* Quest.

**BARADAN** One of the knights who went on the Grail* Quest.

**BARAM** One of the knights who went on the Grail* Quest.

**BARROW** The landing place of Joseph of Arimathea*, according to a chapbook called *The Holy Disciple* (18th Century).

**BEATRICE** M. Aroux proposed that *Beatrice* was the codename of a secret society for which the Grail* was the Gnosticism of Catharism itself. The name seems to be taken from Beatrice, who inspired Dante and appeared in his works. [The Beatrice in question was probably Beatrice di Folco Portinari (1266-90)]. Dante himself was supposed to be one of the group's leaders.

**BECKERY** Formerly a village near Glastonbury*, it has now been swallowed up by the town itself. It is said there was an old oratory here dedicated to Mary Magdalen*. Here St Bridget was said to have come and a chapel was built here for that saint. John of Glastonbury says that it was identical with the

Perilous Chapel*. Arthur* is supposed to have visited there once and found a hermit saying Mass, while the Virgin Mary assisted, offering her Son as a sacrifice for the sins of the world.

**BEDIVERE** One of Arthur's knights, he figures in *Preiddeu Annwn*. His name in Welsh, *Bedwyr*, comes from Celtic *bodowidr*, 'he who knows the grave', a cheerful name if ever I heard one. He was depicted as one-handed. In *Diu Crône* his name was somehow transformed into Nebedons. A. Hunt thinks Bedwyr identical with Nodens* (Nudd). He is pictured here by Aubrey Beardsley.

**BELACANE** Queen of Zazamanc*, whom Gahmuret* rescued when she was besieged by an army of Scots and Greenlanders. The leader of this force was the Scottish king Vridebrant, who was a long way from home. Gahmuret became the father of Fierefiz* by her.

**BENCIN** A servant of Pelles* in the Italian *Tavola Ritonda*. He was related to Perceval*.

**BLACK HERMIT** In *Perlesvaus* the Loathly Damsel* and others were driving a cart containing heads sealed in gold, silver and lead. When they passed the Black Hermit's castle, 152 knights in black came running out and grabbed the heads. Eventually the Black Hermit was killed by Perceval*.

**BLACK KNIGHT** In *Perlesvaus*, a knight with a burning lance who attacked Arthur* and wounded him. This was the only way the lance's fire could be put out. Arthur killed the Knight. His lance shows similarities to the burning lances in Irish mythology and may be akin to the Grail Lance* itself.

**BLACK MADONNA** Some of those who advocate the Bloodline* argument regarding the Grail* hold that the Black Madonna statues of Europe represent Mary Magdalen*. Few historians, however, regard these statues as being other than those of Mary the Mother of Jesus*. Smoke and candle soot over the years may have blackened them. An example is the Black Madonna of Einsiedin in Switzerland. In 1798, because of the Napoleonic Wars, it was moved to Austria for safety. When it was returned in 1803, to the horror of the local priests, it had been given a good cleaning and was no longer a Black Madonna. Knowing the faithful would be outraged, the priests had to blacken it again.

It is, of course, not impossible that some of the statues of the Virgin were originally made out of black wood. It may have been that those who first sculpted the Virgin and Child took as their model sculptures of Isis and the Child Horus.

**BLEHERIS** An authority or source so or similarly named cited by Chrétien and others. His name in Welsh would have been *Bleddri.* There was definitely an historical person called Bledhericus in the 12th Century (mentioned by Giraldus Cambrensis) and he may have been identical with this personage. H. Harrison suggests he was identical with Henry of Blois, none of whose known writings are supposed to have survived. He may actually have brought the Grail* legend from Wales to France and been the one to introduce it to a continental audience. He may also be identical with a personage named Breri who is mentioned in the *Tristram* of Thomas.

**BLEOBERIS** A prominent knight of Arthur's court who took part in the Grail* Quest. During this he was attacked by Arthur the Less*, whom he slew.

**BLIHOS BLEHERIS** In the *Elucidation* the maidens raped by King Amagons* and his followers in due course gave birth to sons who protected them. They lived in the forest. Gawain* in due course overcame one of them called Blihis Bleheris, who told the Knights of the Round Table who they were. One wonders if there is a relationship to Bleheris*.

**BLIOCADRAN** The father of Perceval* in the poem of the same name, which serves as a prologue to the Perceval saga. His wife, after his death in a tournament, raised Perceval in the Waste Forest.

**BLOODLINE** The notion that the Grail* was a bloodline, a dynasty, is one first promoted in the book *The Holy Blood and the Holy Grail* (1982). Henry Lovelich (15th Century) had said that the meaning of the Grail was *Sank Ryal* meaning 'holy blood' rather than 'holy dish' and this gave rise to the idea. This idea was used in the now discredited argument put forward that the Holy Grail was a bloodline descended from Christ. However, the argument was resumed by Laurence Gardner.

Arguments by Gardner for a bloodline and on other biblical matters seem to depend on a contention put forward by Australian biblical scholar Barbara Thiering, which claimed to discover a code in the New Testament which meant it could be read at two levels, by those who were in on the secret and those who were not. Dr Thiering's argument has generally been rejected by biblical scholars. Noted Jewish scholar Geza Vermes says that Thiering's arguments have not been accepted by the academic community and that she misuses the *pesher* system which is the basis of her work. Other scholarly writers who have disparaged her work include N.T. Wright and C.B. Forbes, the latter claiming that her logic was sloppy and that she resorted to wild guesswork. G. Martinez referred to it as science fiction. Gardner contends Jesus* was a dynastic Davidic king who had to be married to his foreordained bride, Mary Magdalene*.

Gardner argues that certain New Testament personages were really the same as other New Testament personages, e.g., Joseph of Arimathea* was identical with James the Just and Simon Magus with Simon Zelotes. He claims the three crucified on Calvary on Good Friday were in fact Jesus, Simon Zelotes and Judas Iscariot and all were alive when taken down from the Cross. Jesus' descendants became known as "fisher kings" because, as a priest of the Order of Melchizedek, he was a "fisher". They became the House of Acqs and the Merovingians* evolved from the Fisher Kings.

As might be expected, biblical scholars generally regard all this with profound scepticism. Much of it is based on a legend that Mary Magdalene and others came to ultimately to France, but this legend is generally regarded as non-historical. *See* **Mary Magdalen**. For how Jesus came to be regarded as an ancestor of the Merovingian dynasty, *see* Merovingians. Gardner's work seems to be part and parcel of supporting a claimant to the Stuart throne of Scotland. He maintains that the Bloodline flowed through the House of Stewart. The earliest known member of this House was one Alan of Dol in Brittany. The family migrated to Scotland. Walter Stewart (1293-1326) married into the royal family and his son Robert eventually became King of Scots. There is no substance to the argument that they are descended from Jesus* and the claimant concerned, Michel Lafosse, is widely regarded as an impostor.

'Texas John', writing in the BBC Wales/North East website, says that while there was a bloodline, Arthur was in it, but it was unconnected with Jesus. Who Texas John may be, I cannot say.

**BOND, FREDERICK BLIGH** (1864-1945) An architect at Glastonbury* who tried to glean information from the reservoir of human knowledge through a medium. His opinion of the Grail* was that it was a spiritual, but not a material, reality.

**BOOK OF THE HOLY GRAIL** A book allegedly written by Joseph of Arimathea* in 54 AD. It was published in 1999, apparently under the aegis of J.R. Ploughman, Patriarch of the Merovingian Gnostic Church. This book claims to be the original source of the Grail legend.

**BORDIGHERA CUP** In 1885, Dr J.A. Goodchild discovered a glass bowl (or cup, as it came to be called) in Bordighera, Italy. It was shaped like a saucer and there was an indication of its possibly once having had a stem. It had on it a design resembling a Maltese cross.

In 1897, while staying at an hotel in Paris, he found he could not move. A voice spoke to him, informing him that the cup had been carried by Jesus*. He was to take the Cup to Bride's Well, in the area of Glastonbury*. called the Women's Quarter. Goodchild always felt the Cup's virtues should be channelled by women.

A voice (?the same one) spoke to him in Glastonbury. He came to Bride's Well, receiving directions as he went, and placed the cup in a hollow in the well.

In 1906, he saw a sign, a sword in the eastern sky. Another sign followed on 3$^{rd}$ September: a cup in the western sky with balls above it.

Meanwhile, Wellesley Tudor Pole (1884-1968) had a vision of Bride's Well.

The Cup was found by the Allen sisters, who replaced it, but was later brought, with Dr Goodchild's consent, to Bristol by their friend Katharine Tudor Pole. There they made an oratory for the Cup. Wellesley Tudor Pole felt it should be attended by women. They held services, conducted by the women, including some baptisms and marriages.

The Tudor Poles seem to have become convinced the Cup was the Grail*. So too did Basil Wilberforce, an Anglican archdeacon. Goodchild held it might not have been the Grail, but might have been carried by Christ. In due course word about the Cup became public. The *Bristol Evening News* wondered if this was something referred to as the Great Sapphire of Glastonbury, mentioned in Henry VIII's time.

The Cup is currently in the possession of the Chalice Well* Trust.

**BORS** In the standard version of the Grail* story found in Malory, Bors is the third of the three knights to achieve the Grail. His youth had been somewhat troubled. The son of the King of Gannes, he was the cousin of Lancelot*, but his father's realm was overcome by King Claudas* (who may be based on Clovis*, King of the Franks). The Lady of the Lake, who was raising Lancelot, set a messenger to Claudas' court who rescued the boys by turning them into greyhounds.

According to the *Lancelot-Grail*, before he actually achieved the Grail, he had already seen it when visiting the castle of Corbenic*. There he saw Elaine* and Galahad*, her little son by Lancelot. He took part in the Grail feast and subsequently saw the Grail, covered with a piece of white samite*, on a silver table, with a man in a bishop's garb kneeling before it. Bors went to the Grail and removed the samite. The room was filled with brightness, but he was warned to approach no further.

Of the three knights who achieved the Grail in Malory, Bors was the only one who was not a virgin. He had been tricked with a magic ring into sleeping with Claire, daughter of King Brandegoris of Stranggore. Their son was Elyan the White, who later became Emperor of Constantinople.

In the Grail quest he joined up with Perceval* and Galahad* and they experienced the Grail together. He eventually returned to Arthur's court.

R.S. Loomis has suggested he derives ultimately from the Welsh mythical hero Pryderi. Pryderi was also called Gwri which became Gohors which, in turn, became Bohort.

**The Attainment: The Vision of the Holy Grail to Sir Galahad, Sir Bors, and Sir Perceval (also known as The Achievement of the Grail or The Achievement of Sir Galahad, accompanied by Sir Bors, and Sir Perceval). , Number 6 of the Holy Grail tapestries woven by Morris & Co. 1891-94 for Stanmore Hall. This version woven by Morris & Co. for Lawrence Hodson of Compton Hall 1895-96. Wool and silk on cotton warp. Birmingham Museum and Art Gallery.**

**BRAN** *see* Bron

**BRANGEMORE**  The woman who built the Chapel Perilous*.  She was buried beneath an altar there.

**BRISEN**  This personage tricked Lancelot* into sleeping with Elaine*, so that he might beget Galahad*.  She also tricked him into sleeping with Elaine on a second occasion.

**BRITAIN**  The country where many of the Grail* adventures occur and over which Arthur* is depicted as ruling.  There was no such realm as England at the time.  Indeed, according to legend Arthur was a leader of the Ancient Britons (ancestors of the modern Welsh, Cornish and Bretons) who were fighting off the ancestors of the English at this period.  Although later sources describe Arthur as King of England, this is an anachronism.

As to the population of Britain before Roman times, they are usually spoken of as Celts.  However, this is more a linguistic than a racial term.  The Celtic culture was supposed to have had its origin at Hallstadt, but in fact the culture found there was widespread and does not indicate whether its members were Celtic speakers.  Modern research now suggests that the Celtic language group first came into existence in the Iberian Peninsula.  DNA testing has shown that 75% of the modern British population are descended from an immigration when the Ice Age receded, between 15000 to 7500 years ago.There was a further influx about 6500 years ago.  These may have been Neolithic farmers who introduced the Celtic speech.  Before the Roman arrival, there may also have been a Germanic influence in Britain.  This would have been caused by the invasion of the Belgae, who Caesar says were part Celtic and part Germanic, but he may simply mean they came from opposite banks of the Rhine.  There may have been Scandinavian incursions in the north of England and Scotland.

The Anglo-Saxon invasions came largely after the Roman withdrawal in the early 5th Century.  They would have been there in the traditional Arthurian period.  It is clear, however, that racially they only formed a small part of the population, the majority of those in their territories being conquered Britons.

This gives us an idea of the composition of the population of Britain at the supposed time of the Grail* quest.

**BROKEN SWORD**  A sword associated with the Grail*.  It was shown to Perceval* in the *First Continuation*, but he could not fix it.  In the *Third Continuation* Perceval took it back to the place of its forging, which was guarded by a brace of serpents.  Perceval slew them.  The smith there repaired the sword.

In the *Second Continuation* Perceval was able to mend the sword, but it lacked a notch.  In the *Fourth Continuation*, this  lack indicated that the sin of letting his mother die of grief still marred his purity.  Perceval set out on his travels again and, when he returned, he was able to effect a complete repair.

In *Peredur* it is Perceval (Peredur*) himself who mended the sword.  It was his own.  He used it to cut through an iron staple twice.  Each time the sword mended itself.  On the third occasion it did not.  According to *Perlesvaus* a Roman emperor called Evalus had placed a sacred stone in the sword.

This sword started its career on Solomon's Ship*.  It was broken and rejoined on a number of occasions; for example, Nascien* broke it fighting a giant and it had to be rejoined by Mordrain*.  What its significance was is unclear.  It seems to have been necessary for it to be joined before the Grail could be achieved.  If one assigns a fertility significance to the entire Grail saga, it may have been a phallic symbol.  Flavia Anderson thinks it was a firebrand.

How Sir Galahad, Sir Bors and Sir Percival were Fed with the Sanc Grael; But Sir Percival's Sister Died by the Way, a watercolour by Dante Gabriel Rossetti

R.S. Loomis draws our attention to the parallel in the Irish *Agallamh na Seanórach* (12th Century) where Caoilte entered an otherworldly house and was asked by Fergus, son of the chief of the Irish gods, to mend a sword.

**BRON** In Robert, we are told he was the brother-in-law of Joseph of Arimathea*. In the course of their travels, he caught a fish which fed all comers. He became known as the Rich Fisher*. He accompanied Peter* to the Vale of Avaron.

Bron may be in origin the British god Bran, if the Grail* is to be assigned a Celtic origin. Just as the Fisher King*, whom we may identify with Bron, the Rich Fisher, is wounded in the thighs, so Bran is wounded in the foot. Both wounds may be euphemisms for castration, laying the land waste because of the king's infertility.

Bran led an expedition to Ireland - probably originally the Otherworld* - just as Arthur* led one to the Otherworld in *Preiddeu Annwfn*, which was probably identical to the one he led to Ireland in *Culhwch ac Olwen*. This was because Ireland had become a euhemerisation of the Otherworld. Both of the stories involved cauldrons*. In *Culhwch*, the Irish had a cauldron into which they could throw their dead, who were at once revived, but could not speak. Only seven warriors plus Bran returned from Ireland, just as only seven warriors returned from Annwn in the Arthurian poem. Bran told his men to cut off his head, though in this state he was still able to be a merry travelling companion. The head was at length buried in London at a place called Gwynfryn, perhaps where the Tower now stands. That Bran was a god rather than a man originally is indicated by the fact he was able to walk across the Irish Sea and use himself as a bridge so his men could cross the Shannon. Just as the Welsh treated Bran as a hero of old rather than a god when they wrote in the Christian era, so they turned the Otherworld, the dwelling of the pagan gods, into Ireland.

There are some parallels between Arthur and Bran. The word *bran* in Old Welsh meant 'raven' (in Modern Welsh it means a crow, while *cigfran* signifies raven; *bran* signifies a raven in both Irish and Breton). In Cornish lore, Arthur is supposed to have turned into a raven rather than dying, though the legend varies, saying sometimes that he turned into a chough or puffin. The purpose of burying Bran's head was to protect the country, but the *Triads* tell us Arthur dug the head up, feeling he could do the task himself. These various factors might lead those who consider Arthur was a Celtic god to conclude he was identical with Bran. The origin of Bran's cauldron seems to have ultimately been a lake in Ireland, presumably really the Otherworld.

It would seem that both Arthur and Bran led expeditions to the Otherworld to find a magic vessel, a cauldron that was the proto-Grail.

The god Bran may be an Irish import into Wales. Ireland had its own story of Bran. The story of *Imram Brain* tells of his voyage westwards, but has limited similarity to that of his Welsh namesake. However, another work, *Immacaldan in Druad Brain* tells how Bran crossed the sea to attack a land and seize a magic treasure. Nevertheless, it has been maintained by Dáithí Ó hÓgáin that the Irish Bran was not a god in origin, but a personage in a fictitious romance, his name suggested by Srúibh Brain in Donegal and that of his father Feabhal by Loch Foyle, between Donegal and Derry.

Brancaster (Norfolk) may be named after the god Bran.

The character Brandegorls of Stranggore, who turns up as a king in Arthurian romance, may spring from the same source. So may Gawain's* grandfather Brandigain, mentioned in the *Second Continuation*. The knight Brandinor, who went on the Grail Quest, is possibly also derived from Bran.

Confusion was to make Bran a Christian missionary. Because one of the chief leaders who opposed the Emperor Claudius when he invaded Britain was called Caratacus (Welsh *Caradog*) son of Cunobelinus and because Bran also had a son called Caradog, he was assumed to be the historical Caratacus' father. When Caratacus was sent as a captive to Rome, Bran was said to have gone with him. Iolo Morganwg claimed he was converted to Christianity. He is said to have returned to Britain to preach along with Joseph of Arimathea*. Gardner's Bloodline* argument asserts Bran was an archdruid and married Joseph's daughter. These stories seem utterly false and, in the case of Iolo, there is the suspicion of deliberate mendacity.

**BRIDALAM** A knight who went on the Grail Quest*.

**BRIDGE OF THE NEEDLE** This bridge led to the Grail Castle* in *Perlesvaus*. It looked needle-thin, but was in fact of normal width.

**BROBARZ** A realm ruled by Condwiramurs*, who, according to Wolfram, was succoured by Perceval*. When he married her, he became its ruler.

**BROWN, DAN** US writer, born Exeter, NH, in 1964. Although writers of modern fiction are not included in this work as a rule, his novel *The Da Vinci Code*, because of a claim that much of its background is true and because it concerns the Grail*, has caused much confusion amongst readers. It states as factual that the Priory of Sion* was founded in 1099 and that Isaac Newton, Victor Hugo and Leonardo Da Vinci were amongst its members. Such assertions warn us to treat Brown as a researcher with great caution. *See also* Bloodline, Mary Magdalene, Cathars.

Fictional works based on the Grail Bloodline* theory also include Liz Greene *Dreamer of the Vine* (1980) and Lewis Perdue *Da Vinci Legend* (1983) and *Daughter of God* (2000).

**BRUGES** Because it contains a relic of the Blood of Christ, this Belgian city is called the City of the Grail*. The Holy Blood of Bruges was brought there in 1149 or later by Count Dietrich of Flanders. There is no documentary evidence for it before 1207.

**BRUMEL** The castle of Corbenic* which housed the Grail* had an adjacent town of the same name. The approach to this was a bridge, which was guarded by the knight Brumel.

**BURROWBRIDGE** According to local lore, Joseph of Arimathea* visited this Somerset location on two different occasions.

# C

**CAERLAVEROCK**  The site of a castle in Scotland, south of Dumfries.  It was built in the 13<sup>th</sup> Century.  P. Coppens has suggested that the Grail Castle* once stood where it stands now.

**CAIAPHAS**  The Jewish high priest, AD18-36.  After the Resurrection of Jesus*, according to Lovelich, he said Joseph of Arimathea* was to be put in a cell and left to starve.  Jesus brought him the Grail*, which sustained him.

**CAIN**  According to Gardner's Bloodline* argument, Cain, the murderer of Abel, was the first king of the Grail* bloodline.  His mother Eve was partially Annunanki* and his father was not Adam but a full-blooded Annunaki called Enki*, thus giving him special blood.  Cain's wife was called Luluwa* and was the daughter of Lilith* and was therefore full-blooded Annunaki.  This made Cain's blood special.  The Bloodline was not interfered with by the Flood, which Gardner places before Adam.

This peculiar story is without value.  Cain (Hebrew *kayin*, smith) is probably the eponymous ancestor of the Kenites, a clan of wandering blacksmiths, who were not Israelitish in origin.

**CALENDIN**  A knight who went on the Grail* Quest.

**CALIGANTE**  A knight who went on the Grail* Quest.

**CALOGREANT**  Variant form of Colgrevance*.

**CAMBERNIC**  A name given to the kingdom lying around the Grail Castle*.  Because it is sometimes called Cambernic Bernicia it is thought it was in the north of England where Bernicia (Welsh *Bryneich*) lay.  It seems to be a variant of Corbenic*.

**CAMELOT**  The seat of Arthur's* court, whose location has excited much surmise.  In the *Estoire* we are told that it was ruled by King Agrestes who underwent conversion by Joseph* and Josephe*, who then departed, leaving twelve disciples in charge.  Then Agrestes made everyone turn back to heathendom, killed the twelve persons Joseph had left behind and went mad.  The populace, greatly perturbed, sent for Joseph and Josephe again, who put things right.

Camelot was also the scene of Arthur's headquarters.  The prefix *cam-* is undoubtedly Celtic.  One suggestion regarding its location has been Colchester, called *Camulodunum* in ancient times, but this would seem to be very vulnerable for a 5<sup>th</sup> Century British capital, bearing in mind that its shores are washed by the

North Sea, over which the Anglo-Saxon invaders came. Another place called Camulodunum in ancient times and therefore a possible contender was Slack (West Yorkshire).

At Cadbury Castle in Somerset there was a hill fort constructed in BC 400. After the Roman withdrawal from Britain, it seems to have been refortified and to have been the seat of an important British ruler. It was far larger than any defensive structure of the period that has yet been discovered. There was a Great Hall there and there also seems to have been a local tradition that it was Camelot. This was recorded by the Tudor antiquarian Leland. In 1998 a bronze-age burial in a coffin shaped like a boat was unearthed here. It was pointing towards Glastonbury Tor*. In D. Cobb's *Mysterious Somerset and Bristol* (2011) the owner of the Camelot Inn in South Cadbury told of hearing many tales of a white horse carrying a knight, perhaps King Arthur, coming down Folly Lane on Midsummer Eve, particularly when that fell on a Tuesday. He himself claimed to have heard hoofbeats. Caves harbouring Arthur and his knights are to be found at nearby Cadbury Camp, in the vicinity of Nailsea. At Cadbury itself are Arthur's Palace and Arthur's Well.

Viroconium, (photographed left in the late 19th Century by Francis Bedford, during the original excavation) whose ruins lie near the village of Wroxeter, has also been suggested, as it was the capital of the powerful kingdom of Powys about 500.

In Malory's *Morte d'Arthur*, which is the version of the Arthurian legends familiar to most English-speaking readers, Camelot is identified with Winchester. The first work in which this identification was made was perhaps Chrétien's *Cligés*.

**CAMLET MOAT**  An island surrounded by a moat in Trent Park, London.

Camlet is in fact a shortened form of Camelot*, its original name, by which it has been known from at least the 15th Century. It has become something of a sacred sight for certain people. A White Lady, who generates a benevolent aura, has been reported there. C. Street, who claims to have seen her three times, suggests she is one of the Grail* Maidens of the wells mentioned in the *Elucidation*.

**CANAAN**  In the *Estoire* he was one of Joseph of Arimathea's* companions. The Grail* refused to serve him and he furiously killed his twelve brothers, while Simeon*, whom the Grail had also refused, wounded Peter*. The Christians buried both malefactors alive.

**CANDELABRUM**  One of the Grail* hallows. N. Gold feels this may have been added to the story, as it was not one of the four treasures of the Tuatha Dé Danaan*. The purpose was to contrast its light with the Grail's greater light.

OPPOSITE: St. Dominic de Guzman and the Albigensians. Panel by Berruguete, 15th century. This portrays the story of a disputation between St. Dominic and the Albigensians (Cathars), in which the books of both were thrown on a fire and St. Dominic's books were miraculously preserved from the flames.

**CARBONEK**  Anglicised form of Corbenic*.

**CARCELOIS**  One of the Grail Kings*.

**CAREMBAUS**  A knight who went on the Grail* Quest.

**CASTEL DEL MONTE**  A castle built by the Holy Roman Emperor Frederick II (reigned 1194-1250) in south-eastern Italy.  It was not built for human habitation, nor does it seem to have been built for defensive purposes.  Legend suggests it was once occupied by the Grail*.  The castle is now a World Heritage Site.

**CASTLE DORE**  A hill fort in Cornwall.  There is a tradition that the Grail* was kept there for a time.

**CASTLE OF MAIDENS**  Galahad* freed maidens who were being held captive by seven brothers in this castle in the course of the Grail* Quest.  The brothers were later slain by Gawain* and other knights.

**CASTLE OF THE CESCLE D'OR**  This castle was held by the Knight of the Burning Dragon, according to *Perlesvaus.*  This knight had a dragon on his shield which actually spurted fire.  Perceval* rescued the castle.  The Cescle d'Or was Christ's Crown of Thorns, which was awarded to Perceval.

**CASTLE OF TREACHERY**  During the Grail* Quest, this castle was conquered by Galahad*.

**CATHARS**  A religious breakaway group which throve in France, recorded from the 11th Century AD and also called Albigensians, because one of their centres was the town of Albi.  Their success was in part due to shortcomings in the Catholic clergy.

The origin of their doctrines was Gnostic, having come originally from the East.  The contention has been made by sundry modern writers that they knew about the Grail Bloodline* and protected the Jesus* dynasty.

Cathars held the Gnostic notion that there were two gods - the God of Jesus and the God of the Old Testament.  The latter was termed in Gnosticism the Demiurge and was cruel and evil.  It was he who had created the world and that matter, of which the world was made up, was evil.  Human spirits were imprisoned in matter.  Therefore, human reproduction was evil, as it brought more matter into the world.

Bearing this idea in mind, it seems extremely unlikely that they should be custodians of any dynasty/bloodline of any kind, which brought new matter (children) into the world.  A violent crusade was launched by the Pope against them after a papal legate was murdered in 1208.  This included the Siege of Montségur*, which some have identified with Montsalvaesch*, Wolfram's Grail castle, but which was in fact constructed by the Cathars from ruins after Wolfram's poem had been written.  Many of those fighting on the Cathar side were in fact Catholics.

Victory for the Crusade meant that the French king could tighten his hold on southern areas of France, over which he had had only loose control before, so he was all in favour of hostilities.

The undoubtedly high moral code of the Cathars was one of the reasons they were so successful. That they nourished a hidden dynasty, bearing in mind their doctrines of the flesh, seems incredible. By the end of the 14th Century, no Cathars appear to have been left.

L. Olschi had the theory that the scenes in the Grail Castle* depicted by Chrétien were intended to be a portrait of Cathar worship, forsaken by Perceval, who is then introduced to true Catholicism by his uncle. However, those in the Castle were eating meat, while Cathars were largely vegan, though some ate fish.

The Cathars were first associated with the Grail in 1937 when an organisation called *Les Amis de Montségur et du Saint-Graal* was formed.

**CAULDRON**   (Welsh *pair*)  In a couple of stories of Arthur* questing for cauldrons we may have the origin of the Grail* stories, for we are dealing with a search for a vessel, sometimes providing food in a manner reminiscent of the Grail. These tales, which are Celtic, possibly come directly from Celtic mythology. The stories of Arthur seem to be variants of stories of Bran*.

The cauldron seems to have figured as a major object in Celtic religion. Cauldrons were used for ritual purposes. In the tale of *Branwen*, Bran went to Ireland* with his army. It is supposed by some that in this case Ireland may stand for Annwfn*, the Otherworld*. This was a substitution made in Christian times, as the Otherworld had been a dwelling place of gods. There occurred a battle with the Irish, who had a magic cauldron, which revived any dead person thrown into it. Only seven survived the expedition.

Bran and Arthur seem in some respects to have been closely identified.

In the poem *Preiddeu Annwfn*, Arthur led an expedition to Annwfn, which seemed to be with a view to capturing the cauldron of the chief of the Otherworld. Only seven survived the this raid. A duplicate of this adventure seems to be Arthur's expedition to Ireland in *Culhwch ac Olwen* to capture a magic cauldron. Here, as in the story of *Branwen*, Ireland has apparently been substituted for the Otherworld. In both these works it is stated that the cauldron would not cook the food of a coward.

It seems that Celtic Britain harboured a tradition of a journey to the Otherworld to capture a wondrous cauldron. This may have been the Cauldron of Britain of which Manawyddan* was said to have been perpetual guardian. Ceridwen*, though depicted as a human, was probably a goddess in origin and she too had a divine cauldron. The seizing of the cauldron may have been the prototype of the acquisition of the Grail.

In the Celtic mythology of Ireland, similar cauldrons featured and may have influenced the Grail story. The chief of the Irish gods was the Dagda, who had a marvellous cauldron that satisfied every group who ate from it. The Dagda appears to be identical with Donn, the god of the dead, who was probably regarded as presiding over the Otherworld. The worlds of gods and ghosts were considered identical. Another term applied to the Dagda was Da Derga, the red god. In Da Derga's hostel was a cauldron perpetually used and never removed from the fire. A Brythonic equivalent of Da Derga may have given rise to such personages as the Red Knight* and the Red Giant* of the Grail tradition. An alternative to Da Derga seems to have been Da Cóca, whose name also means the red god. Perhaps he was related to the British god Cocidius (Welsh *coch*=red). Thus we have in Irish myth a red god (Da Derga, Da Cóca) with a cauldron of plenty (Da Derga, Dagda) who lives in the Otherworld (Donn). It would seem this red god is a sun god. Similarities to elements in the Grail story are obvious. Thus the seizure of the cauldron may have been a pan-Celtic motif.

N. Gold holds the cauldron was nothing supernatural, but a symbol of sovereignty and, if Arthur* held it, it would enhance his power. He also feels a cauldron was part of the coronation ceremony of the king, a vessel in which the monarch had to be placed. Whatever about that, cult vessels like the Marlborough Vat (*ca.* BC 50) emphasise the importance of the cauldron cult in Britain.

F. Anderson has argued that a concave mirror could have been the cauldron of Celtic lore.

**CELIDOINE** The son of Nascien*. Imprisoned with his father by Galafre, when the former was carried off by a cloud, Galafre determined to fling Celidoine from the battlements. Nine hands, apparently with no other corporeal features attached, caught him and saved him, while Galafre was struck by lightning. In due course Celidoine landed on an island where he converted King Label to Christianity. When the king died, his subjects, far from converted, put Celidoine adrift in a boat. The king's daughter, however, was to turn up again. He found Solomon's Ship* and boarded it and rescued Nascien* from an island. Later King Label's daughter joined them. A man in a white robe who walked over the water told Celidoine to depart from the others in a boat. When the party arrived in Britain, they met Celidoine once again at a castle called Galafort. He eventually married King Label's daughter.

While the word *celidoine* means celandine in early English, the name of this hero was concocted as an eponym for Caledonia, the Latin name for Scotland. R.S. Loomis has suggested his name and perhaps some other matters concerning him have been derived from Merlin* Celidonius, as Merlin was said to have gone mad in a Scottish wood.

**CELTIC CHURCH** A term used to signify the form of Christianity in Britain, Ireland and Brittany at the time of the Arthurian sagas. However, although it differed liturgically from Continental Christianity, it did not differ in doctrine and was not regarded as a separate denomination, either by its members or the Papacy. Thus, for example, the Celtic Fergal, who latinized his name as Vergilius, became Bishop of Salzburg. There was an Irish monastery as far east as Kiev in the Ukraine. The major differences between the Celtic and Latin rites were the dating of Easter and the tonsure worn by monks. This tonsure may have been inherited from the druids. It is referred to in Latin as *tonsura magorum*. It was also somewhat organisationally different, with the main emphasis being on the monastic rather than the diocesan. Again, this does not imply heresy.

The Celtic Church is sometimes wrongly called the Culdee Church. Culdees were monks and hermits (sometimes laymen) who took their name from Irish *Céili Dé* (companions of God). They were found in Ireland, Scotland and York. They were not, as has been stated elsewhere, a fusion of the Druids and Essenes.

This is the church background against which any historical Grail* Quest would have taken place.

**CELTIC GODS OF BRITAIN** There can be no exhaustive list of the Celtic gods worshipped by the Ancient Britons, for the very good reason that many may be unrecorded. It is, however, the case that, with the coming of Christianity, many were euhemerised, that is to say, they were demoted from gods to persons who supposedly lived in Britain in early times. It is even reasonable to argue that Arthur* was one such, although there is no record of a god so called.

Some of those who occur in the Grail* legends may well have been Celtic gods in origin. One of these gods, Beli Mawr, (below left) was regarded as an ancestor in several pedigrees of Celtic rulers. His name may be a shortened form of *Belenos*, a god who was worshipped widely on the Continent, his cult spreading from Aquitaine to Austria. I should add that Beli has no connection with the Phoenician god Baal.

Beli seems to have been an important god in the Celtic pantheon. His wife was Dôn, who, if she is to be identified with the Irish Dana/Anu would seem to be the mother of the gods. Beli and Dôn were the parents of Arianhrod and Beli also had a daughter called Penarddun.

Beli is assigned in the *Mabinogion* sons called Llud, Caswallaun and Nynnio and also Llefelys. In Lludd we have an alternative name of the god Nodens*. Pedigrees make Afallach, from whose name some derive Avalon*, his son. Modron (a British form of the goddess Matrona, the goddess of the River Marne) was Afallach's daughter.

Arianhrod was the mother of Dylan (who was probably a sea-god) and Lleu Llaw Gyffes (equivalent of the Irish god Lugh and the Continental Lugos).

Beli may have found his way into Geoffrey as Heli, the father of Cassibellaunus, Lud and Nennius, whose names bear close resemblances

to the sons of Beli. This Heli (whose name was not unknown in Wales and Brittany at this time) is depicted as an ancient British king. A late legend said the island of Ely was named after him. That at least some Britons held Beli to be the chief of the gods is suggested by the fact that Britain was sometimes referred to as *Ynys Vel Veli* (Beli's Honey Isle). He is given different fathers which may be because of a vagueness of tradition indicating that in the original myth he had no father whatsoever.

Beli is sometimes said to have been the father of Anna, cousin of the Virgin Mary. However, if Dôn was the equivalent of Irish Dana, perhaps she had another name like Anu, the alternative name of that goddess, and she was Christianised by turning her into Anna.

Having spoken of these gods, we must now ask where they might arise in Grail legend. Beli would seem to be Pelles* or Pellehan*. He was also called Beli Mawr which may have turned into Pellinore*. He had, moreover, a powerful spear, reminiscent of the Grail Lance*. However, there is a suggestion made, first by J. Rhys, then by J. Carey that Pwyll, another Brythonic god, was the true original of Pelles. Carey further suggests that in Pryderi, his son, we might seek the original of Perceval. Modron developed into Morgan Le Fay* in Avalon. Her father Afallach may be the source of King Evelake*, though P.C. Bartrum doubts this, despite its being the opinion held by Sir John Rhys. Bran*, a god from another family, becomes Bron*.

The whole Grail scenario may be some kind of initiation ritual, Peredur*/Perceval* standing the initiate and the night in the Perilous Bed* representing the ordeal undergone.

**CERIDWEN** She is mentioned by Welsh poets and may be a goddess in origin. She is associated with a cauldron*, but whether it is the same one which may be a prototype of the Grail* is uncertain. It was a cauldron of inspiration and was intended for her son Afgaddu, to compensate for his bad looks. However, Gwion, a child, consumed drops from the cauldron and acquired the inspiration. Then the cauldron blew up. Gwion kept turning himself into different animals and Ceridwen did likewise with a view to swallowing him. This she did and subsequently gave birth to him as Taliesin*. This is found in a late story, *Hanes Taliesin* (16th Century).

It is possible that a cauldron which was a proto-Grail* may well have conferred inspiration.

Ceridwen's cauldron certainly features in Welsh poetry. Taliesin is also connected with the proto-Grail cauldron. Many think Ceridwen (painted here by Christopher Williams in 1910) was a goddess, but it has also been argued that she was merely a witch in Welsh fairy lore. This is the opinion of Ronald Hutton, whose earnest face is so often seen on our television screens. He feels she was made into a goddess by the Gogynfeirdd, Welsh poets of the 12th-14th Centuries. Ceridwen was reputedly

married to one Tegid Foel who lived in a valley now occupied by Llyn Tegid (Bala Lake). Tegid's name is Latin - it is the Welsh form of *Tacitus* - so he can hardly have been a British god. However, he may have been ritually married to Ceridwen as the tutelary goddess of his realm.

**CHALICE WELL**  A well in Glastonbury* (opposite) in which it is said the Grail* is or once was. The water is reddish due to iron content and this may have led people to associate it with the blood of the Eucharist. It was once known as Bloody Well. Its original name seems to have been Chalk Well and it may have been given its present appellation with the Grail in mind. Just when this happened is uncertain. The nearby Chalice Hill is called "a ground called Challice" in a 1716 document and the Well has borne its present name since at least 1751.

According to legend, Joseph of Arimathea buried the Grail here and red water sprang up from it. A. Roberts holds that the well was dug by astronomer priests, who arrived about BC 2000. The well does not dry up, even in drought.

**CHAMPIONS OF THE RICH HOUSEHOLD**  In the *Elucidation* we are told that certain maidens who dwelt in wells were removed by evildoers. After a time, numbers of knights also emerged from these wells and became a band of malefactors.

**CHAPEL OF THE GRAIL**  This was situated in the 19th Century in a house called Fairview in Onecote (Derbyshire). It was owned by an eccentric personage, Sir Ralph de Tunstall-Sneyd (1862-1947). It was said he was descended from Alfred the Great. He called himself a Knight and Bard of the Round Table and regarded himself as a seeker of the Grail*. In September, 1926, this worthy presided at an Assembly of Druids at Thor's Cave in the Peak District. He used the title Chief Bard of the Imperishable Sacred Land. A further assembly was held in 1927. Those taking part wore black and white robes.

**CHESS**  In Perceval's* quest for the Grail*, a number of sources involve chess matches. Thus, in the *First Continuation* Perceval played chess against an invisible person, who defeated him. Perceval was about to throw the board away in a tantrum, but a beautiful girl arose from the moat and asked him not to. In the German romance *Diu Crône* our attention is drawn to two youths playing chess in the Grail castle, while a chess match also turns up in *Peredur*. There is also a magic chessboard in the romance of *Perlesvaus*. The pieces were of ivory and gold. Gawain took the ivory side and the gold pieces themselves played against him. As Gawain was losing, he smashed the game.

That the chess episode of the Grail Quest was important seems certain, but the nature of its importance seems to have been forgotten. The present writer suspects that, if the original tale comes from a Celtic source, the actual game played was not chess but gwyddbwyll, a Welsh game which at times seems to have had a mythical significance. It is probably equivalent to the Irish *fidchell*, supposedly invented by the god Lugh. Gwyddbwyll has equivalents in Cornish (*gwedhboell*) and Breton (*gwezboell*). We know little about how it was actually played, but each side seems to have had an equal number of pieces. One of the legendary Thirteen Treasures of the Island of Britain was the Magic Gwyddbwyll Board of Gwenddolau, where the pieces would play by themselves. N.R. Mann suggests it was a ritual competition for sovereignty*.

The mystic significance of the game is shown by the fact that Chrétien places at the entrance to the Grail Castle* a man carving a piece of wood. This would seem to go back to a Celtic mythological figure called Eudaf, who carved chessmen at an otherworldly hall in Welsh legend. He had a rich chessboard. Owing to linguistic misunderstanding, Chrétien changed the woodcarver into a man with an artificial leg and therefore no connection with chess is associated with him. (We are not told what he was carving)

This Eudaf in Welsh genealogies is the grandson of Bran*, from which we can deduce he may have been a god. He is given the adjective *hen,* 'old'. Historical Welshmen of prominence, however, also revered Bran as an ancestral deity. Eudaf may have been one of those. Geoffrey latinises his name as Octavius.

**CHEVALIERS DU SAINT-GRAAL** A modern esoteric order with headquarters in Nova Scotia.

**CHILD IN A TREE** A curious being whom Perceval* encountered in the *First Continuation.* Seeing this child sitting on a branch, Perceval asked him for directions to the Fisher King's* castle. The child, holding an apple, said he could not answer and ascended the tree, at the top vanishing like the boy in the Indian rope trick. The actual meaning of the episode cannot be discovered or, if it can, it hasn't been.

**CHRÉTIEN DE TROYES** French poet, who wrote a number of Arthurian poems. He flourished in the 12th Century, but details of his life are obscure. U.T. Holmes has suggested he was a Jew who had converted to Christianity. He wrote a number of Arthurian romances, notably *Perceval*, the first Grail* romance. Chrétien probably used as his sources details picked up from Breton poems and/or tales. These in turn would have been carried to Brittany, whither many Celts from Britain had betaken themselves.

The Breton language of today is related to Welsh and Cornish and more distantly to Irish, Scottish Gaelic and Manx. Apart from its being a vessel of some sort, Chrétien does not tell us what the Grail actually is and he left the poem unfinished. Four other poems attempted to continue the story.

The *First Continuation* and its sequel, the *Second Continuation,* were both penned about 1200. The author of the second may have been one Gautier de Donaing. Two sequels were written to the *Second Continuation.* These are referred to as the *Third Continuation* (by Manessier) and the *Fourth Continuation* (by Gerbert), but they do not follow each other: both follow the *Second Continuation* independently.

**CHRISTIC GRAIL LINEAGE** According to Dunford, this seems to have originated in a fusion of the lineages of Japhet and Shem*, sons of Noah. When the Celts and Hebrews cross fertilised, a Grail* lineage came into being.

This was managed in two ways. It was carried first by Scota and then by Tea [2 *syl.*]. In the early Middle Ages the term *Scotti* was applied by the Romans to the Irish. They, in turn, developed a mythical ancestress, Scota, the daughter of Pharaoh, who married Míle, a Celtic leader, and died in battle in Foley's Glen, Kerry. In later years, when the Irish kingdom of Dalriada extended into Scotland, the word *Scotti* was applied to the inhabitants of that country and in English it was called Scotland. In the 14th Century the claim was made that Scota came directly to Scotland. Scota is not regarded as an historical personage.

An Irish legend featured Tara, the seat of important and later paramount kings of the country, as having been founded by Tea. This was based on a false etymology. Tara (Irish *Teamhair*) means a place of vantage, but certain early writers surmised it came from *Teamhúir* (house of Tea), thus bringing Tea, a chimerical personage, into existence.

In 1872 one J.B. Bartnette surmised that the legendary Irish king Ollamh Fodla was none other than the prophet Jeremiah and a story grew up that he brought Hamutal, widow of King Josiah of Judah, and the Stone of Destiny to Ireland. A variant is that he brought Tea, the daughter of King Zedekiah to Ireland. In this way it has been suggested the Hebrew lineage was combined with the Celtic.

None of these stories is based on genuine Irish legend or is in the least historical. Some of this material was once favoured by the British Israelites.

**CHURCH OF THE HOLY GRAIL** A church in Tréhorenteuc in Brittany. It is dedicated to Saint Onenne, who lived in the 6th-7th Centuries. A king's daughter, she became a gooseherd. Her geese made such a noise when she was once attacked that local people came to her rescue. Her intercession is invoked with regard to eye illnesses. In the 20th Century Abbé Gillard (1901-79) added many decorations, including stained glass windows, to the Church relevant the Holy Grail. He was helped by Karl Rezarbeck (painter) and Jean Delpeche (glassmaker). On a stained glass window to the back is a depiction of Christ about to give the Grail to Joseph of Arimathea*. The church is full of Grail and Arthurian themes. It is about 40 kilometres from Rennes.

**CLAMACHIDES** In the *Estoire*, a knight whose severed hand was restored when he touched the shield of Mordrains*.

**CLARISCHANZE** A Grail* Maiden in Wolfram.

**CLINSCHOR** *see* Klingsor

**CLOVIS I** (died 511; date uncertain) According to the *Holy Blood and the Holy Grail* he was part of the Grail* Bloodline*.

He was King of the Franks and may be the prototype of the King Claudas of Arthurian romance. The latter makes his first appearance in *Perlesvaus*. However, Clovis became a Christian only in 496, before which time he had been a pagan, which hardly qualifies him as a member of a Christian Bloodline. He is pictured opposite in 'Clovis roi des Francs' by François-Louis Dejuinne (1786–1844)

**CODIAS** A knight who went on the Grail Quest*.

**COLGREVANCE** A minor Arthurian knight who sought the Grail*. When he tried to intervene in a fight between Bors* and Lionel*, he was killed. A variant version has him killed after the quest by Lancelot*.

**CONDWIRAMURS** Wife of Perceval* in Wolfram. She bore him two sons, Loherangrin (better known as Lohengrin*) and Kardeiz. Perceval had first fallen is love with Liase, daughter of Gornemant, but had then mistaken Condwiramurs for her and so fallen in love with Condwiramurs.

**CONN** Mythological King of Ireland, in origin a god. He was the ancestor-deity of the Connachta, who ruled central and western Ireland. His supposed grandson was Cormac mac Art, who may actually have been a prehistoric king. Their adventures contain incidents reminiscent of Grail* stories. In time, their tales may have spread to Britain and, in modified form, reached France *via* Brittany. In the case of Conn, he underwent a *baile,* a word which might be translated as a frenetic trance leading to inspiration.

The Book of Fenagh renders the term as *furorem spiritualem*. Conn is told by Sovereignty* that he and his descendants will rule Ireland. In the same way, a Grail* maiden may have offered the cup of rulership to the Grail hero, the Grail itself being such a cup. *See* Sovereignty.

The two sources for Conn's vision are *Baile Chuinn Chéadchathaigh* (?7th Century) and *Baile in Scail* (? 9th Century).

**COPPER CASTLE** In *Perlesvaus*, a castle guarded by two copper men, in fact robots, though that word had yet to be invented. They wielded iron mallets. Perceval* defeated them. The inhabitants of this place were evil and the River of Hell was nearby.

**CORBENIC** The Grail Castle*, built specially to house the Grail* by King Alfasein in the land of Listenois*. In due course, an enchantment was placed on the castle which meant you could reach it only by accident. R.S. Loomis suggests it comes from Old French *cor benit*, 'blessed horn', meaning a horn of plenty. The Grail Castle* is first so named in the *Lancelot-Grail*. The town of Corbeni (Latin *Corbiniacum*) and the monastery of Corbie in France have been suggested as possible origins of the name. In addition, there was an Abbot of Corbie named Mordrains* from 769-781. N. Gold feels the name came from Welsh *Caer Bannawc*, 'horned castle'.

Regarding the ultimate fate of Corbenic, legend says it may have been destroyed hundreds of years later by Charlemagne.

**CORBU, NOEL** (1912-68) A restauranteur who bought the estate of Berenger Saunière* in 1946. There he opened a restaurant in 1955. He appears to have been the source of a journalist A. Salomon who related a story in *La Depeche de Midi* on January 12th, 1956. In this it is alleged that Saunière discovered, while conducting repairs in the Church, the treasure of Blanche of Castile. Parchments in Latin, which no one other than Saunière himself could read, were also discovered. He also told him that Saunière's secretary had implied she would give him access to a huge sum of money after her death. While there is no mention of the Bloodline* in this, it has been used by proponents of the Bloodline theory to show that Sauniere had access to information about it which earned him vast sums of hush money.

**CORRYVRECKEN** This place name means 'the cauldron* of the plaid' and it is a terrifying whirlpool off the west coast of Scotland, between the islands of Jura and Scarba. This swirls when the Atlantic tide is running. It is caused by an underwater pillar of rock. Because of the usage of the term 'cauldron' to describe it, G. Strachan has suggested that it is the cauldron which is the prototype of the Grail*. It is associated with the mythological Cailleach Bheur (blue hag), who seems to have been a goddess of winter in origin. She was said to wash her plaid in the cauldron. The whirlpool itself is called An Cailleach, indicating it was regarded as a place of worship of this goddess. Nearby are the ruins of buildings without obvious function and they may have formed a religious centre. H. MacArthur has suggested that *Preiddeu Annwn* may represent an historical episode and that Arthur* actually led an expedition to Corryvrecken. He also suggests that Caer Sidi, visited in the poem, was on Scarba.

**CORSAPIN** The vavasour of Nascien*, who at length joined Joseph of Arimathea* in Britain*. His son Elicanor came with him.

**CRAIDANOS** A knight who went on the Grail* Quest.

**CRINIDES** A knight who went on the Grail* Quest.

**CRUDEL** A British king who captured Joseph* and Josephe*. They were rescued by Mordrain*.

**CULDEES** *see* Celtic Church

# D

**DAMATAL** An evil knight who attacked Galahad* during the Grail* Quest. Galahad wounded him sorely.

**DAMCAB** One of the knights on the Grail* Quest.

**DE CHÉRISEY, PHILIPPE** (1923-85) A hoaxer who was a confederate of Pierre Plantard* and who manufactured the parchments which are referred to in the *Dossiers Secrets* in the Bibliothèque Nationale. He admitted this in 1967, 1975 and 1978 and it was confirmed by a manuscript he left after his death entitled *Pierre et papier.* In this he tells us the parchments were a joke.

**DE SÈDE, GERARD** (1921-2004) The author of the book *L'Or de Rennes* (1967) producing reproductions of forged parchments intending to substantiate the claims of the Priory of Sion*. His son dismissed the longtime existence of the Priory as nonsense ("absolute piffle").

**DEMANDA DEL SANTO GRAAL** Spanish version of the Grail* story, published at Toledo in 1515.

**DEMANDA DO SANTO GRAAL** Portuguese Galician version of the Grail* story (15th Century).

**DESPOSYNI** The term comes from Greek *desposunos*, 'of or belonging to the Master'. A term used in the early Church for relations of Jesus*, first surfacing in written record in the work of Julius Africanus (3rd Century). While such relations existed, they cannot be used to validate the argument of the Bloodline*, as there is no mention of their being descendants of Jesus. Despite this, it has been quoted by Bloodline advocates.

**DIANA, PRINCESS OF WALES** According to J. King and J. Beveridge, she was a Grail Queen (an exceptional member of the Judaic Grail Family*) who presented a danger to the Windsors and Freemasons and may have supported a Merovingian-Stuart restoration. There was also opposition to her marrying a Muslim. The two authors claim this led to her being assassinated.

*See also* Grail Family (King and Beveridge).

**DIDOT-PERCEVAL** Grail* romance of the 13th Century. It comes from a manuscript which was privately owned by a man named Didot. This is now in the Bibliothèque Nationale. There is another copy in the Biblioteca Estense, Modena, which is reckoned superior. There are differences in the MSS. which indicate that both are defective copies of an original.

**DINADAN** One of the knights who went on the Grail* Quest, in the course of which Agravain a Mordred* killed him. The image below is by Aubrey Beardsley and is entitled: "How King Makre a Sir Dinadan heard Sir Palomides makeing great sarrow and mourning for La Beale Isoud."

**DINAS BRAN** A steep hill near Llangollen (Denbighsire) with a medieval castle at the top. However, previous to that there was a hill fort here, perhaps dating to BC 600. The name means 'Castle of the Crow', but it must be remembered that Bran also designates an ancient Celtic god, who seems to have been the prototype of Bron*, the Fisher King*. It may have been the original Grail Castle*. It was also called Corbyn, reminiscent of Corbenic*, the Grail castle's name. It is known in English as Crow Castle. Nearby you have Gorsedd Fran (throne of Bran) and Llyn Bran (Bran's lake). There is a tradition that the Grail is in a cave beneath it.

**DISGYL** A dish which was one of the Thirteen Treasures of the Island of Britain. While it was ascribed in a later text to Rhydderch Hael, King of Strathclyde in the 6th Century, older sources speak of two vessels belonging to one Rhegennyd, a person of scholarly bent. These were both a dish (*dysgl*) and a vat (*gren*). In *Peredur* the decapitated head was carried on a dysgl, which, in meaning, is the same as grail in its original significance. Thus it could be said to equate to the Grail* in the Grail Procession*.

**DIWRNACH** In *Culhwch ac Olwen* an Irishman, owner of a cauldron*. To help Culhwch win the hand of Olwen, Arthur* had to procure this. When Diwrnach refused to supply it, Arthur had to lead an expedition to Ireland to obtain it and they carried it off successfully. It was said it would not boil the food of a coward and the same was said of the Otherworld* cauldron in *Preiddeu Annwn*. This would indicate that we are dealing here with two versions of the same story. In *Culhwch* the Otherworld of the gods has been turned, for Christian ears, into Ireland.

The name of this character may come from an Irish personage named Dorn. This was a woman in an Irish story who found a magic cauldron of truth. In a later version Dorn was a man.

An alternative suggestion is that this is a Welsh form of the Irish name Tigernach.

**DOLOROUS STROKE** The blow which caused the land to become a Wasteland*. The story as narrated by Malory is that Balin* struck Pellam* through the thighs with the Grail Lance* causing the country round about to wax infertile. Only the asking of the Grail Question* could restore the Grail King* to health and the land to fruitfulness.

In Celtic religious belief, the productivity of the land was tied up with the welfare of the King. If the King had a physical defect, the land would suffer. The wound of the King through the thighs is generally taken to be an euphemism for castration and the land in consequence of its infliction became a desert. In this story there is every likelihood we have the medieval version of a Celtic myth.

**DOSSIERS SECRETS DE HENRY LOBINEAU** These documents consist of 27 pages. They were deposited in the Bibliothèque Nationale in 1967. They contain false genealogies saying Pierre Plantard* was descended from the Merovingians*.

**DRAGON COURT** An organisation which, if I understand aright, claims to be composed of descendants of antediluvian Grail Kings* who have special DNA which gives them the right to rule the rest of the human race. Their sovereign is a man called De Vere.

**DUNSTANBURGH** A castle in Northumberland. Although the present structure dates from the 14$^{th}$ Century, there is evidence of prehistoric occupation of the site. According to legend, the Grail* is buried here, guarded by a knight called Sir Guy the Seeker.

**DUPLICATE GRAIL** This was kept at Constantinople according to the *Jungerer Titurel*.

**DUR** *see* Sumer.

**DYABIUS** In the *Queste* we are told that he was a servant of Pelles*. He was related to Perceval*.

# E

**ECTOR**  The half-brother of Lancelot*. He had a fight with Perceval* and both would have died had not the Grail* healed them. This character should not be confused with Arthur's* foster-father in Malory's *Morte d'Arthur*.

**EDEN**  This is given as an alternative name for the Grail Castle* and it is worth seeing if there is any such place name in Britain which might be its locale.

Castle Eden, a village in Co Durham, is supposedly the site of a lost castle. King Arthur* and his knights' ghosts are said to be seen in daytime in the village disguised as chickens. Beneath the lost castle Arthur and his knights are said to lie sleeping. Arthur was said to have walked through Castle Eden with his head shaven. His hall was said to have been on the banks of the village. A pathway leading from Old Shotton Hall is supposed to be Arthur's hunting route. At Wingate Slack lights are reported at night: they are said to be the eyes of Arthur's knights. St James's Church contains a statue of a monk into which Merlin* is supposed to have turned himself. Although none of this specifically relates to the Grail Castle, its many Arthurian associations indicate it is possibly the Eden intended.

The River Eden in Cumbria has next to it the wobbly ruin of Pendragon Castle, supposedly built by Uther, Arthur's father. No definite record of a building on the spot exists before the 12th Century. However, again the Arthurian associations may indicate it was once associated with the Grail Castle.

There seems to be no Arthurian association with Eden Castle in Aberdeenshire.

**EFRAWG**  Father of Peredur* in the Welsh romance of the same name. It is actually a title, meaning 'ruler of York' (Latin *Eboracum*). As there were historical twins called Peredur and Gwrgi ruling York in the 6th Century, this Peredur is likely to be the one in the romance. However, it has been suggested that the territory their father actually ruled was Wroxeter and nearby areas.

Sir John Rhys holds the opinion that Efrawg was not originally a place name or a title, but rather the personal name of a god, from which the place name was derived.

**ELAINE**  In Malory, the daughter of Pelles* who bore Galahad* to Lancelot*. She is not so named elsewhere; possibly Malory was confused by the name of Elaine of Astolat, who died of love for Lancelot. Elsewhere she is called Helizabel, but is popularly known as Amite.

A major problem here is that if she is the destined mother of the Grail* knight, why so non-Christian a

ploy is used to arrange Lancelot's copulation with her? This possibly hearkens back to a pagan version of the Grail story, as there is a suspicion that Pelles is an euhemerisation of the Celtic god Beli Mawr. In the original' perhaps Perceval/Peredur is the warrior concerned. This might mean Pelles' daughter was in origin a goddess. If so, she was probably not known by the name Elaine.

N. Gold is sure the sundry Elaines in Malory, whether they appear in the Grail* story or others, are in origin the same person and are also to be identified with Blanchefleur*. He further identifies them with Elyan the White*, a male Grail quester.

**ELIAZAR** Son of Pelles*. The name is also found as *Eleazar.* He was made a knight by Gawain*.

**ELYAN THE WHITE** The son of Bors*. By the use of a magic ring, Bors was tricked into sleeping with Elyan's mother, Claire. The story is so similar to that of Lancelot's* begetting Galahad* by sleeping with Elaine* that one is bound to wonder if the two stories are not variants of each other. Claire was the daughter of King Brandegoris of Stranggore, who may be identical with the god Bran*, just as Pelleas*, the father of Elaine, seems to be identical with the god Beli Mawr*. There is room for further investigation here. Elyan ended up as Emperor of Constantinople.

**ENKI** A god of the Sumerians, known to the later Akkadians as Ea. According to the Babylonian epic *Enuma Elish* mankind was created by Enki, the first man being Adapa. L. Gardner believed Enki to be the ancestor of Cain*, whom he held to be the progenitor of the Grail* Bloodline*.

**ENYGEUS** In Robert, she was the sister of Joseph of Arimathea* and the wife of Brons*. The meaning of the name is not known, but P. Imbs has suggested a Greek origin, *eugenes*, 'well-born'. A connection with Irish *inghean*, 'daughter', has also been suggested.

**EREC** The hero of a romance by Chrétien. We are told in the *Post Vulgate* that he went on the Grail* Quest. He was a Breton hero in origin and may have been an historical personage, the founder of the small Breton kingdom of Bro-Weroch.

**ESCLAMOR** A gigantic knight who took part in the Grail* quest.

**ESTOIRE DE SAINT GRAAL** A romance of the 13th Century, part of the Lancelot-Graal cycle. It deals with the adventures of Joseph of Arimathea*.

**ESUS** *see* Hesus.

**EVELAKE** King of Sarras*. The *Estoire* tells us he was showing signs indicating he should convert to Christianity, but he failed to do so. As a result, he was defeated by King Tholomer* of Egypt. In a second battle he was joined by his brother-in-law, Seraphe*. After this, Evelake was baptised, taking the name of Mordrain*. Similarly, Seraphe was baptised as Nascien*. Lovelich informs us Evelake had trouble dealing with the concept of the Trinity, but then had a dream in which he saw a tree with a single stock and three trunks, which enabled him to understand the doctrine more.

Mordrain was carried away by the Spirit of the Lord when his palace was struck by a thunderstorm and ended up on a rock in the middle of the sea. He was visited by a man in a silver ship who offered him bread, then a lady in a dark ship who urged him to accompany her. This scenario was repeated a number of times, Eventually he went aboard the silver ship and set off. Later on he boarded Solomon's Ship* in which he found Nascien* ensconced. He mended the sword which Nascien had broken fighting a giant.

Mordrain went to Britain subsequent to the others, as a result of a vision of Jesus*. He rescued Joseph* and Josephe* from King Crudel*, but lost his eyesight for coming too close to the Grail*.

Centuries later, Galahad came on the sick Mordrain, which at last permitted him to die.

In the French romance *Histoire de Grimal* Evelake had a son before his migration to Britain. This was Grimal, who became King of Babylonia.

The suggestion has been made that Evelake was in origin the British god *Afallach*, who was supposed to have given his name to Avalon* and been the father of Modron, who later developed into Morgan Le Fay.

**EWOA** A Celtic wife of Joseph of Arimathea*, according to material allegedly accessed from the Akashic Record* by occultists.

# F

**FARAMUND** A legendary king of the Franks. He may never have existed, but according to legend he was the son of Marcomir. The historian Sigebert of Gembloux in fact says Marcomir was the first king. Gregory of Tours places Faramund's reign in 420. L. Gardner in his Bloodline* theory makes Faramund a Fisher King* through whose veins ran the holy blood and whose father was Frotmund*. This hardly ties in with his being Marcomir's son, but the website "Ancestors of John Savile" says Frotmund was in fact a woman who was married to Marcomir and she was identical with Frimutel*.

**FELIX** A knight on the Grail* Quest.

**FERTILITY RITE** Some would hold that the Grail* ritual was in origin a fertility rite over which a Christian veneer has been daubed. In pagan belief it was often held that the health of the land was bound up with the health of the king. Thus in early Ireland we learn that the king had to be without blemish. The Maimed King* is wounded through the thighs and this is generally taken to be an euphemism for castration, rendering him infertile. The land round about is desolate, sometimes this desolation encompassing the whole of Britain. Only the Grail Question* can heal both king and country. When Gawain* visited the Grail Castle*, he asked only one of the three necessary questions and, as a result, the land was partially, but not wholly replenished. He was also unable to mend the Broken Sword*, which might also have had phallic connotations.

Perceval* asked the correct question and the entire Wasteland* was renewed. J.L. Weston suggests that behind the Grail mystery lay the pagan rite of Adonis, which, after the establishment of Christianity, had to be held in secret. She suspects the Fisher King* and the Maimed King, whose identities are somewhat confused, were originally different, the former being the priest of the cult, the second the god. Proponents of this theory would see the Grail Lance* as phallic, while the Grail itself would represent female generative organs.

While a fertility element seems likely to lie behind the story, it does not correspond very closely to that of Adonis. In Greek myth, Adonis was a youth, beloved by Aphrodite. He was killed by a wild boar. Zeus, however, allowed him to return to earth in the summer, but he had to stay in the Underworld in the winter. The return to earth of Adonis is not mentioned before the 2$^{nd}$ Century AD. However, such a myth was told already about the Greek Persephone and the oriental god Tammuz.

**FIEREFIZ** In Wolfram, the son of Gahmuret* by Belacane* and therefore the half-brother of Perceval*. Wolfram was not sure what a mixed race child would look like, so he made Fierefiz piebald. When the lad grew up he came to Europe to find his father. He and Perceval met and fought, but then discovered they were brothers. Fierefiz became a Christian to enable him to see the Grail and ultimately married Repanse de Schoye*. They became the parents of Prester John*.

**FIRST CONTINUATION** *see* Chrétien de Troyes.

**FISHBOURNE**  Site of a magnificent Roman villa, built by Cogidubnus, King of the Atrebates, in the south of England. V.P. Jones suggests that a remnant of this may have been the castle of the Fisher King*.

**FISHER KING/MAIMED KING**  These two characters have become so muddled that a single article devoted to them seems more useful than separate ones. Basically, as a result of the Dolorous Stroke*, which involved the piercing of the Maimed King's thighs, the land round about and possibly the whole of Logres* has become infertile. It is necessary to ask the Grail Question* for the Grail to heal the King and with him the land.

In the *Estoire* the King received his wound fighting at Rome. In the *Queste* he received it when he drew the sword on Solomon's Ship*.

The problem lies in the fact that there are at times two kings, one more of an invalid (the Maimed King) than the other. Both, however, seem to be wounded. The Maimed King, according to Chrétien, is fed by the Sacred Host, which is carried in the Grail, but the Fisher King is the one who should be asked the Grail Question*. When Perceval* visits there is an ancient invalid in the background. In Chrétien he first encounters the Fisher King in a boat. Since his wound, all he can do is catch fish. In the *Lancelot-Grail*, the Maimed King is Pellam* or Pellehan*, the Fisher King his son Pelles*.

In Malory we are told Balin* wounded Pellam, which would make him the Maimed King and Pelles the Fisher King; but the Fisher King is also called by Malory a king distinct from Pelles. In Robert Bron* is called the Rich Fisher* for catching a fish for Joseph*.

As the reader will see, the whole question is very confused, but the present writer suspects there was originally just a single king whom storytelling and manuscript transmission transformed into more than one. R.S. Loomis feels the king concerned may in origin be either the god Bran* or Manawyddan. They may have originally been seen as the same deity, splitting into two persons.

In Wolfram Titurel* occupies the position of the Maimed King and his grandson Amfortas* that of the Fisher King, but

Within the castle of the Grail, Amfortas is brought before the Grail shrine itself, and Titurel's coffin. He cries out to his dead father to offer him rest from his sufferings, and wishes to join him in death ("Mein vater! Hochgesegneter der Helden!") The Knights of Grail passionately urge Amfortas to uncover the Grail to them again but Amfortas, in a frenzy, says he will never again show the Grail, commanding the Knights, instead, to kill him and end his suffering and the shame he has brought on the Knighthood. At this moment, Parsifal steps forth and says that only one weapon can heal the wound ("Nur eine Waffe taugt"): with the Spear he touches Amfortas' side, and both heals and absolves him. ("Parsifal")

Amfortas is also maimed.

A. Stone feels that the Fisher King is mythical, representing a Welsh adoption of Odin. This is not far-fetched, as the Belgae, who may have been Germanic, invaded Britain before Caesar. They could have brought Odin, under the name of *Woden, Wotan* or the like, with them. Just as the Fisher King was castrated, so apparently was Odin, for he had the term *jalkr*, 'gelding', applied to him.

U.T. Holmes, who proposes a Jewish origin for much of the Grail story, would identify the younger king with Jacob and the elder with Abraham. M. Beckett feels the Fisher King (*Roi Pescheor*) was possibly the *Roi Pecheor* (Sinner King) standing for humanity awaiting redemption. It may be that the god behind the Fisher King is Nodens. A temple of this god has been discovered at Lydney Park (Gloucestershire), 3888 square metres/4800 square feet in extent. A depiction of the god shows him as a triton facing a fisher catching a salmon with a hook. T.F. O'Rahilly supposes that both fisher and salmon are forms of Nodens, so the Grail myth was originally applied to him. This temple was constructed in 365 AD.

*List of wounded kings:-*

Bron*, Evelake*, Lambor*, Pellehan*, Pelles*.

**FISHER'S HILL** Hill in Glastonbury* at the eastern end of Wearyall Hill. It is said that this was the site of the Grail Castle*.

**FLEGETANIS** A descendant of King Solomon, who, according to Wolfram, had found the secrets of the Grail* in the stars. These he wrote in Arabic. Wolfram asserts that Flegetanis worshipped a calf. The secrets were supposedly found by Kyot, whom Wolfram claimed as a source. One recent source has gone so far as to identify Flegetanis with Hiram Abiff, who, in a Masonic fable, was murdered for not divulging secrets. This Hiram Abiff worked on Solomon's Temple.

**FLEGETINE** Daughter of the King of Midian, she was the wife of Nascien* and mother of Celidoine*, who joined them in Britain.

**FLORIE OF LUNEL**  A Grail* damsel in Wolfram.

**FOLIE PERCEVAL**  A supposed romance of Perceval*, which is said to antedate Chrétien and be perhaps the original Grail* romance.  However, it seems to be a non-existent work.  It is said to be in the Bibliothèque Nationale, but the authorities there can find no trace of it.  No major Arthurian scholar seems to know anything about it.

**FORT KNOX**  A military base in Kentucky which contains the heavily guarded U.S. Bullion Repository.  Such are the security regulations that no one other than the Mint Police is allowed in.  A 2 kiliton nuclear warhead could not penetrate the door of the vault.  According to legend, the vault contains a room which harbours the Holy Grail* and the Ark of the Covenant*.

**FORTINGALL**  A village in Perthshire, Scotland.  According to alleged Akashic Records*, Joseph of Arimathea went there with a band of followers.  It was the seat of the Christic Lineage*.

**FOURTH CONTINUATION** *see* Chrétien de Troyes.

**FRIMUTEL**  In Wolfram, Perceval's deceased grandfather.  His father, Titurel*, was still alive when the action of the poem took place

# G

**GADRAN**  A knight who went on the Grail* Quest.

**GAHMURET**  In Wolfram, the father of Perceval*.  He was the son of King Gandin of Anjou, whose brother, Galoes, inherited the throne.  He first married Belacane, Queen of Zazamanc*, but abandoned her.  She later gave birth to his son Fierefiz*.  He then married Herzeloyde*, by whom he became Perceval's father.  R.S. Loomis suggests the tale of Gahmuret and the romance *Bliocardan* may share elements taken from the same source.

**GAIS LE GROS**  Perceval's* grandfather in *Perlesvaus.*

**GALAHAD**  This name first appears in the *Queste* and was made up by its authors, who appear to have been Cistercians.  The Grail* legend was a strange multifaceted thing and they wished to make a thoroughly Christian version of it.  The name is in Old French *Galaad*, which is identical with the Latin for the biblical *Gilead.*  A former theory that he had a Welsh prototype called *Gwalhafed* is now discounted: the names are unrelated.

The story of Galahad's conception will be dealt with below.  Suffice it at this stage to say he was the son of Lancelot*, who knighted him.  He was supposed by the writers to be a kind of Christ-like figure.  Indeed, at one stage in the poem he is told by an oldster that he resembles Christ, but lacks his nobility.  It has been conjectured that the philosophy of the Cistercian Order influenced the shaping of his character.

We are told that when Galahad arrived at Arthur's court he sat in the Siege Perilous*.  He also drew a sword from a block of marble in the river, which had defied other efforts.  He was now the best knight in the world and would deliver the land from desolation.  This seems to imply that the whole of Logres* had been rendered a desert.

The Grail now appeared, supplying foodstuffs for everyone.  The Knights of the Round Table determined to set off on a quest to find it.  In previous accounts of the Grail (except for *Diu Crône*), the hero had been Perceval, but in the *Queste* version and Malory's version derived from it, this distinction would now fall on Galahad.

As he went a-questing, Galahad was approached by a squire called Meleagant, carrying a shield that hitherto none had been able to wear without being killed or wounded.  Galahad was accompanied already by a hermit.  A knight in white armour appeared.  He narrated the history of the Grail to Galahad and

then vanished. In due course, Galahad and Meleagant parted company, but later Galahad had to rescue his erstwhile companion from attack and bring him, wounded, to a hospital.

Galahad was now travelling with Owain the Bastard* and Dodinel*. They parted company, Galahad following a White Stag*.

Galahad was subsequently attacked separately by Gawain* and Bors*. The reason seemed to be these knights were wearing their vizors down and didn't recognise each other. It seemed to be accepted practice that, if you saw an unknown knight, you charged him first and asked questions afterwards. Gawain was wounded. Galahad killed Bors' horse, but happily then recognised his foe, so he stayed his hand. It was tough luck on the horse, however.

Galahad and Bors joined up and brought the wounded Gawain to the castle of a king. The king had a daughter of fifteen summers who tried to seduce Gawain, but he rejected her. She killed herself in despair. Bors, who had slept through all this, woke up and the two companions fought off the knights of the castle, who attacked them. The issue was resolved by a single combat between Bors and the king, Bors winning, so he and Galahad were allowed to leave.

Galahad came to the Castle of King Pelles*, the Grail King*, but he left it unrecognised.

One night when Galahad lay sleeping he was wakened by Perceval's sister*, who needed his help. Her cousin had gone mad. Galahad healed her. Perceval's sister stayed with him, but nothing untoward occurred. Galahad was the essential virgin knight. He healed a leprous woman by letting her don his hair shirt. Then he and Perceval's sister hied them to the coast, where they joined Perceval and Bors. They boarded a ship which contained the bed of King Solomon* and a sword. Galahad took the sword and, as the belt had seen better days, Perceval's sister made him a belt from her hair. The sword became known as the Sword of Strange Hangings*.

This helpful female, however, was soon to leave them. They came to a castle where the lady of the castle was a leper. Perceval's sister allowed the inhabitants to drain her body of blood, that the lady might be cured and died in consequence.

King Mark of Cornwall, familiar to those who know the *Tristan* romance, decided to invade Logres* while the knights were away, looking for the Grail. Galahad and the others went to help Arthur, whom Mark was besieging in Camelot*. Mark was defeated and his later plot to poison Galahad was unsuccessful.

Eventually, Galahad, Perceval and Bors reached the Grail Castle. They found that Josephes*, the son of Joseph of Arimathea*, in remarkably good condition for a man of several centuries, was there. He was brought in on a throne, apparelled as a bishop and carried by angels. The Holy Grail appeared on a table of silver. There was a pause, as Josephes stood before the altar. Then the door opened noisily and in came his angelic bearers once more, two carrying candles, one a cloth of red samite* and the last a lance, from which fell drops of blood into a cup the angel held. The candles were positioned on the table, the cloth beside the Grail and the Lance over the Grail, so that the blood fell into it. Josephes took a host from the Grail and raised it and a Child of

bright countenance entered it and it took human form.

Josephes vanished. The knights timorously sat at the table and Christ rose from the bowl. He addressed the knights and gave them the Host. Galahad was to heal the Maimed King* before they left for Sarras*, whither they were instructed to go. They took the Holy Grail to Sarras. The heathen king Escorante imprisoned them there. They were sustained by the Holy Grail for a year. Then, when King Escorante died, Galahad was made king in his stead. After a year he died and a hand came down from heaven with removed the Grail.

Malory tells us that Galahad was buried by Perceval next to Perceval's sister.

John Hardying said Perceval brought back Galahad's heart, encased in gold, to Glastonbury*, where it was buried.

Although Galahad himself is undoubtedly a Christian invention, the story of his begetting can hardly be reconciled with Christian ethics and may be a Celtic story in origin, adapted from the birth of some other hero. We are told that his mother was Elaine*, King Pelles'* daughter and once Lancelot* visited the castle. Pelles knew that Elaine and Lancelot were destined to be the parents of the Grail hero, so he tricked Lancelot into sleeping with Elaine - he thought she was Guinevere in the dark - and thus Galahad was engendered. This story seems so thoroughly unchristian that an investigation into its origins might repay further study. *See* Elaine.

The family tree of Galahad is rather strange:-

The first Galahad was renamed Lancelot and became a king; his son, King Ban, married Elaine; his son, Galahad, was renamed Lancelot* and was the father by Elaine* of Galahad, the subject of this article.

What lies behind this family tree one can only conjecture. It has been suggested that it reflects a pagan custom, but it must be borne in mind that Galahad was invented by writers of a thoroughly Christian stamp.. Perhaps someone with a name similar to Galahad played a part in this tradition. One thinks perhaps of the similarly named *Galaholt*, who occurs elsewhere in Arthurian tradition.

A Galahad son of Joseph of Arimathea* was given the land of Hocelice to rule over. It was later called *Galles* (Wales) after him. So too was *Galafort*, where he was born.

A. Jackson thinks Galahad was a king of the Britons who succeeded Maelgwn* Gwynedd. Such a position is untenable.

**GALAHAD'S MIRACLE** This was actually an abbey. It was called Uther Pendragon Abbey, but, when Galahad survived an attempt by King Mark of Cornwall to poison him there, the name was changed.

**GALES** The father of Perceval* in the *Fourth Continuation*. The name may be simply taken from *Galles*, meaning Wales.

**GALIADIN** A knight on the Grail* quest.

**GALICIA** According to legend, Galahad* came to Galicia in Spain and took a sword from a cliff. Defeating a dragon, he was given golden spurs by a damsel. He went into a church and offered his sword to a chalice, which was identified as the Grail* with the Holy Blood in it.

**GALOSCHES** In the 13th Century romance *Sone de Nausay*, the hero, Sone, went to aid King Alain of Norway, who was faced with attack by the Scots, whose forces boasted a formidable giant. He and the King went to the island of Galosches (which did not produce protective footwear) but where there was a monastery. There they found the Grail*, the body of Joseph of Arimathea* and that of his son Adan* and the Holy Lance. In this romance, Joseph had been the Fisher King* and, when he was wounded, took up fishing as a hobby. The abbot of the monastery donated Joseph's sword to the visitors, which they used against the invading Scots. Sone married Odee, the daughter of King Alain.

An interesting footnote is that the romance tells us that Logres* was the original name of Norway.

**GANDIN** The name of Perceval's* grandfather in Wolfram, taken from a place-name in Styria. His wife's name was Schoette. The River Gandine was named after him.

**GANOR** The first ruler in Britain* whom Joseph of Arimathea* converted to Christianity, according to the *Estoire.*

**GANSGOUTER** The owner of the Castle of Wonders in *Diu Crône[1]*, a magician whose sister fed the Grail* ruler once a year.

**GAR** A knight on the Grail* Quest. He was known as Gar of the Mountain.

**GARNALDO** A knight on the Grail* Quest.

**GARSCHILOYE** A Greenlandic Grail* maiden in Wolfram.

**GAWAIN** Gawain was portrayed as a doughty but courteous knight in Arthur's* court. He was Arthur's nephew, the son of Morgause, wife of King Lot of Lothian. In the Continuations to Chrétien, we are told he came to the Grail Castle* where he saw the Grail Procession*. He asked what the Lance* signified, but fell asleep before asking about the other items in the Procession.

He had also been asked if he could fix the Broken Sword*, but had been unable to do so.

In the *Queste* at the outset Gawain was warned not to proceed by an ugly woman who said that, in the course of the adventure, he would kill nineteen of his fellow knights. Gawain ignored this and came to the Grail castle where he saw tables with persons sitting at them. There entered a beautiful girl carrying a chalice. As she passed each table, it was filled with food. However, Gawain was so struck by the damsel's beauty that he failed to

1. Diu Crône (The Crown) is a Middle High German Arthurian poem of about 30,000 lines, dating from around the 1220s and attributed to Heinrich von dem Türlin. The poem tells of the Knights of the Round Table's quest for the Grail but differs from the better-known "Percival" and "Galahad" versions of the narrative: it is Sir Gawain who achieves the sacred object.

Of the author little is known though it has been suggested that he was from Sankt Veit an der Glan, the capital city of the Duchy of Carinthia in his time.

pray and received nothing.

When the guests withdrew, Gawain found himself on his own. A dwarf came to attack him with a staff, but Gawain disarmed him. The bed in the room had the somewhat discouraging title of the Perilous Bed*. He was warned by a damsel to seize arms before he lay on it and a fiery lance struck him in the shoulder, when all he wanted was a good night's sleep. Then, in due course, someone withdrew the lance. The next peril was a dragon with a cavernous mouth. From this came five hundred young dragons, then in came a leopard. Leopard and dragon fought. Then there was a fight between the old dragon and the young dragons until all were dead. Twelve damsels entered, then a large knight. He and Gawain fought until both were exhausted and they collapsed. Then the palace shook, thunder roared and lightning flashed, but it did not rain. Strange meteorological conditions, if you ask me. Gawain then heard singing, which he felt was of a spiritual nature. Before it, a damsel came in and placed the Holy Grail* on a silver table. Afterwards, she removed it. Gawain was left in the dark, but his shoulder was healed.

He was taken and placed in a cart. When he awoke, he found the cart was of an unpleasant sort and a thin nag drew it. (His own horse followed behind). A damsel with a scourge drove the cart, while interested bystanders threw rubbish at the unfortunate knight it harboured. Then the damsel set him free.

In one Grail romance, *Diu Crône*, Gawain is actually the hero who achieves the Grail. This tells us he arrived at the castle with Lancelot* and Colgrevance*. Within he saw an old man on a bed. Large numbers entered the hall at eventide and a youth came in and laid a sword before the king. All three knights were offered drinks and only Gawain said no. The others accepted and were rendered senseless.

Two damsels came in carrying lights, then two knights with a spear, then two maidens with a toblier* and finally the most beautiful of all women ever with a box and an attendant maid, crying. The woman produced a piece of bread from the box which she broke and one piece was given to the old man.

Gawain asked the Grail Question*. Everyone rejoiced, but it transpired they were all ghosts, except the woman with the Grail and her attendant.

M. Godwin argues that Gawain was the original Grail hero.

Gawain is an Arthurian character taken from Welsh tradition, where he is called *Gwalchmai*. This name may mean 'hawk of May' or 'hawk of the plain' (Welsh *gwalch*, 'hawk'; Celtic *\*magos*, 'plain'). According to Arthurian lore, he returned to Arthur's court and was killed fighting Mordred's forces. He seems to have been particularly popular in the north of England.

**GEOFFREY OF MONMOUTH** (12th Century) Norman-Welsh writer who composed the *Historia Regum Britanniae* and the *Vita Merlini*, both featuring considerable Arthurian matter and having an influence on subsequent Arthurian literature. Neither mentions the Grail*, however.

It is thought that much of the material in his history sprang from his own imagination and he is not a trustworthy authority. He may have taken some of his history from stories of British gods, transformed into heroes of the days of yore.

**GERBERT** *see* Chrétien de Troyes.

**GHIBELLINES** A faction in Italy who opposed papal power politically in the Middle Ages and who championed the Hauhenstaufen Dynasty of the Holy Roman Empire. They were opposed by the Guelphs. J. Evola (1898-1974) felt the Grail* was based on the Ghibelline ideology.

**GIRALDUS CAMBRENSIS** (died 1222) The Welsh writer who mentions the supposed excavation of Arthur's grave at Glastonbury* and who identifies Glastonbury with Avalon*. Pictured left.

**GIRONA** A city in Catalunya/Catalonia which is supposed to harbour a secret society of women guarding the Grail*. There seems to be a sort of ritual involved which is said to have enabled Salvador Dali to enter another dimension.

**GLAESTINGSBURH** Place in Gwynedd, Wales. Blake and Lloyd, who try to place Arthur's* whole realm in Wales, argue that this was the original Glastonbury*.

**GLASTONBURY** A town in Somerset, population 8,800. R. Warner in *A History of the Abbey of Glaston* (1826) felt it likely St Paul had preached at the site. Joseph of Arimathea* is said to have come here, bringing the Grail*. This he is said to have buried at Chalice Well*. According to a letter in the *Central Somerset Gazette* (7th August, 1936) signed 'Glastonian', there was a druidic college there before the coming of Christianity. There seems to be scant evidence for this, but many subsequent writers state it. It was the site of a huge and prestigious abbey in the Middle Ages. It was said St Patrick, after his mission to Ireland, found hermits there and under him they became a community. The Abbey, (photographed below by Nick Redfern) however, never listed the Grail amongst the relics it claimed to harbour, even though this would have led to a vast intake of money.

Various track ways laid in the area in prehistoric times have come to light, notably the Sweet Trackway,

which dates from BC 4000. Also to be found are the Abbot's Trackway of BC 2500 and the Meare Heath Trach dated at BC 1500. Islands grew up, made by incoming waters from the Bristol Channel. These were inhabited and dominated by hill forts. There were also lake villages at Glastonbury and Meare. There was a trade route connected with the Mediterranean in the 1st Century BC. Glastonbury was a focal point for trackways stretching as far as the Midlands. C.A. Raleigh Radford (1900-1999) argued there was a Celtic sanctuary here in pagan times, bounded by the rampart known as Ponter's Ball.

Visible from the town is Glastonbury Tor*. A strange atmosphere is supposed to surround the Tor and this may also stretch as far as the town. John Michell remarks that an otherworldly atmosphere prevails around the Tor. He says that for primitive tribesmen it may have performed the function of a sacred mountain.

Whether the abbey is Celtic or Anglo-Saxon in origin is uncertain. Some argue that the earliest known abbot was the Anglo-Saxon Haemins (7th Century). However, it cannot be ruled out that there was a Celtic monastery here. An abbot named Worgret, possibly unhistorical, is mentioned. Whitehead maintains the headship of the church in Britain was transferred from the Isle of Wight to Glastonbury in 65 AD. Before the inception of monasticism, isolated hermits may have dwelt on the site. The monks' tradition claimed St Patrick as the abbey's founder, though whether it was the apostle of the Irish or another saint of the same name is uncertain. John of Glastonbury produces a legend that there were always twelve hermits living there. There may have been a community on the Tor before the abbey was established on its present site. The Abbey was placed under Benedictine rule by St Dunstan in 943. The town grew up around the abbey. It was in existence by 1086, but may have been considerably older.

William of Malmesbury said the Old Church at Glastonbury was the oldest he knew of in England. The floor was inlaid with polished stones. The paving stones were laid by design in triangles and squares and sealed with lead. He said if he believed some holy secret reposed beneath it, he did no injustice to religion. He also spoke of documents that claimed disciples of Christ had built the Old Church.

A *Life of St Dunstan* written by someone who signed himself merely B said the first neophytes of Christianity were directed here to a church dedicated to the Virgin Mary and consecrated by God, apparently in the sense of Jesus*, himself. William of Malmesbury said St David came to dedicate the church, but Jesus told him in a dream he had already dedicated it to his mother. St David built an extension. John of Glastonbury said the church had been founded by Joseph of Arimathea and eleven disciples, who built the structure of wattles, and Christ dedicated it to himself and his mother. John calls Glastonbury the New Jerusalem. On the other hand, Rhygifarch's *Life of St David* says David founded the church.

A dreadful fire destroyed the Abbey in 1184. Subsequently the grave of King Arthur* was found in the Abbey grounds. Though many regard the discovery as a hoax, this is by no means certain. Arthur is supposed to have been taken to Avalon* after his final battle. After the discovery, Avalon is identified with Glastonbury, but this may not always have been the case.

Beneath Glastonbury are supposed to lie subterranean structures. A tunnel is said to lead from the Abbey to the Tor and there is said to be a hollow space inside the Tor itself. When Henry VIII closed down the Abbey, he had the abbot, St Richard Whiting, and two other monks hanged on the Tor, making it a ghastly imitation of Calvary. This occurred in 1539. Whiting's ghost is said to walk up Dod Lane. Ghostly bells have been reported from the Abbey since 1911.

Glastonbury, Joseph of Arimathea and the Grail have long been connected in the public mind. Whether there is any truth in the legends, one cannot say with certainty. C. Twrga deplores certain things he regards as taking from the mystery of Glastonbury, such as the industrial park and sewage works.

**GLASTONBURY THORN** A thorn brought to Glastonbury by Joseph of Arimathea* according to legend. The tree pictured below is the thorn on Wearyall Hill which had its branches cut off by vandals in 2010.

It is first mentioned in the poem *Here Beginneth the Life of Joseph of Arimathea* (1520). The poem says the Thorn Tree was on Wearyall Hill and bore leaves at Christmas. Dr Layton attested to the fact it bore leaves at Christmas in 1535. It had two trunks in the time of Elizabeth I, but a puritan cut one down and would perhaps have cut the other, but a chip from the tree put out one of his eyes and his leg was cut.

Cuttings from the tree came to be placed in private gardens, but the original tree was cut down by a Roundhead.

An innkeeper in 1715 said the Thorn came from a staff carried by Joseph of Arimathea. According to legend, he had been given land by Arviragus*, he placed the staff in the ground and it blossomed. It is said he planted it on Christmas Day.

There are various descendants or supposed descendants of the Thorn in Glastonbury today. They blossom at Christmas and Easter. One of them, on Wearyall Hill but was vandalised in 2010. However, pagan horticulturist Peter Frearson has replanted it and it began to show new buds in March, 2011.

This extraordinary tree adds to the story of Joseph, also reputed to have brought the Grail* to Britain.

The tree's scientific name is *Crategus monogyne* 'Biflora'.

**GLASTONBURY TOR** A pear-shaped hill, composed of sandstone, 518'/158m high and covered in grass, except for an eroded area, probably the work of animals. Artificial terraces go around the Tor. Their purpose cannot be determined. They may be simple lychets, structures made for agriculture. They

GLASTONBURY AND THE TOR.

could also have been carved with some more mystic end in mind. They may, for example, have been the pathway of a maze. The idea that the Tor had a pre-Christian religious significance is widely known and it is generally regarded as one of the mysterious, perhaps otherworldly, sites of Glastonbury. St Collen is said to have encountered the Celtic god Gwyn ap Nudd on the summit. Two springs there are the Blood Spring which flows through Chalice Well* at the base of the Tor, its water tinged with red, caused by iron and another spring called the White Spring. According to legend, it once emerged from the Tor. There are a number of stones on the Tor. One is called the Living Rock. It is broken in two. There is a tradition of a stone or stones that were once at the top of the Tor.

A church of St Michael was built on top of the Tor but was destroyed in an earthquake in 1275. A second church lasted until Henry VIII displaced Catholicism. Now only a tower remains.

Some believe there are many underground passages in the Tor. There are even those who would hold it is completely hollow. A tradition says that once thirty monks in the Abbey grounds happened to find a tunnel. It led towards the Tor and they went into it. Only three returned - two mad and the third dumb.

The website www.glastonburygrove.net claims some legends say that Arthur* or Merlin* is sleeping beneath the Tor or that Joseph of Arimathea* is there, guarding the Grail*.

About 1956 two boys or young men who lived nearby are said to have entered a cave leading towards the Tor. When they emerged they could not describe what they had seen.

In the limestone under the Tor there may be caves carved out by the water.

K. Knight has said there may once have been stone circles on the north of the Tor. Anthony Roberts, supporting this, notes the presence of the nearby Stonedown Hill. Legend says there is an underground tunnel from the Abbey to the Tor and that other tunnels join it.

There have been reports of UFOs over the Tor and of panic attacks experienced by at least one climber. These may be due to geological factors. Coloured balls of light are often seen around the Tor. A policeman reported eight of them in formation in 1970. There was another report in 1980.

Glastonbury Tor is a Scheduled Ancient Monument.

**GLASTONBURY WALNUT TREE**  A tree said to have grown from a staff planted by Joseph of Arimathea*. It would bud on the 11th June, but never before. This was the feast of St Barnabas.

**GLASTONBURY ZODIAC**  Katherine Maltwood when illustrating *The High History of the Holy Grail*\* in 1935 decided that the exploits in the story reflected zodiacal figures which could be traced in the layout of the landscape in the environs of Glastonbury*. Her scheme has been modified by Mary Caine as follows:-

(a)   *Aries* is depicted as a lamb, its head outlined by the town of Street. The figure is two miles long. Ivyhall to Marshall's Elm represents the forefoot of the Ram. It stands for Gawain*.
(b)   *Taurus* depicts a bull's head and forefront. The back of the bull's neck is Collard Hill. The bull has a third horn at Hood Monument.
(c)   *Gemini* is shown as a child or baby, the head at Dundon Hill, the chest at Lollover Hill. There is an Iron Age hill fort at Dundon Hill.
(d)   *Cancer* is a ship.
(e)   *Leo* is an heraldic lion near Somerton. The lion's mane is at Copley Wood, its chest and stomach

at the River Cary. The lion's back is Somerton Lane and Somerton is between its paws. There is a Red Lion pub in Somerton.

(f)     *Virgo* is an ancient female, the River Cary showing the profile.

(g)     *Libra* is a dove at Barton Saint David.

(h)     *Scorpio* is a four-legged scorpion with a sting at West Lydford.

(i)     *Sagittarius* is a man regarded as King Arthur with a horse. The head is at Catshan. Its tail is at Arthur's Bridge.

(j)     *Capricorn* A goat, its back the road from Glastonbury to Shepton Mallet. Maltwood accidentally identified a haystack as the eye of the goat.

(k)     *Aquarius* represented by a phoenix or an eagle. The wings and head follow the contours of the Tor. An error in the calculation is that a wing of the Phoenix* was a road around Glastonbury made in 1782. There was no road there before. The Chalice Well* is at the end of its beak.

(l)     *Pisces* Two fish and a whale. One fish is Wearyall Hill, the other the town of Street. The whale stretches from Hulk Moor to near Wallyer's Bridge.

(m)     *Argo Navis* replaces Cancer. It is to correspond with Solomon's Ship*. There is a distinct problem with this sign, however: it was made by building rhynes when the moors were drained between 1790-1820. It wasn't there in the Middle Ages.

An additional sign, not regarded as part of the Zodiac, is the Girt Dog of Langport. It is named after a dog in a Somerset wassailing-song. Its tail is at a place called Wagg. Perhaps, it has been speculated, it is there to guard the Zodiac. Another such dog has been discerned by Janet Roberts: she calls it the Polden Hound.

On Dundon Beacon in the Zodiac there was a group of trees which, when photographed from the air, looked like the face of Christ. The trees have now been felled. Merlin* is said to be buried at the centre of the Zodiac at Park Wood.

It is said that the winter signs are in the north and the summer in the south of the Zodiac. There are four main hero figures - Arthur, Gawain*, Lancelot* and Perceval*.

The only trouble with the Glastonbury Zodiac is that it is not discernable by everyone. It has been suggested that you have to be told it's there before you can make it out. Katherine Maltwood claimed to have seen it, but, as an artist, she may have been inclined to see patterns in things. However, it is not impossible that it was made with the cognoscenti in mind. There are, however, problems with some sites, as delineated above. In addition, some people claim to see the shapes of the figures differently from others.

The Zodiac was said to be the original Round Table, meant to depict the round world and the planets. The *Queste* says the Round Table had fed 4000 people and 150 bulls. It was situated in a meadow. A. Roberts feels it was made by a culture antedating all others at Glastonbury, sometime between BC 10,000 and BC 2700. D. Cyr has suggested, in accordance with a theory proposed by I.N. Vail in 1874, that there was once a canopy of cloud surrounding the earth. In this, suggests Cyr, the Zodiac might have been reflected.

C. Evans-Günther, well known to Arthurian enthusiasts, is sceptical about the whole existence of the Zodiac.

**GNOSTICS** Early Christian heretics; for their beliefs *see* Cathars.

**GOLDEN CUP** This belonged to Arthur* in the English *Sir Perceval*. It was stolen, leaving both Arthur* and his land enfeebled, by the Red Knight*, who in due course was slain by Perceval, who donned his armour. When Arthur got the cup back, he regained his former vigour. The cup here fulfils the rôle of the Grail*, on which the vigour of king and country depended.

**GOLDEN POT OF MANNA** This was kept in the Ark of the Covenant*. U.T. Holmes says it was the Grail*.

**GOLDEN VESSEL** In *Perlesvaus* Gawain found this in the midst of a forest. He came upon a fountain with marble pillars adorned with jewels. Attached to the central pillar with a silver chain was a golden vessel. A statue that seemed alive dived into the water. Gawain was going to drink from the vessel, but a voice warned him to refrain. A young priest in white robes, his arm in a sling, poured water from the Golden Vessel into one of his own. Three beauteous maidens appeared carrying bread in a golden vessel, wine in an ivory one and meat in a silver one. They offered these to the Golden Vessel. As they walked away, they merged into one. The peculiarities of this story make it seem as though it may have in origin been some kind of variant of the Grail* story. It contains the vessel, wounded or injured imbiber and the maidens. Their strange union at the end reminds us that in Celtic mythology, goddesses often became triplicate, having once been singular. An example of this would be the Matronae, who had once been a singular Matrona and who later in Britain evolved into Morgan Le Fay*.

**GOON DESERT** Perceval's* uncle in the *Third Continuation* where Partinal killed him with the Broken Sword*. His castle was called Quingragan.

**GORNEMANT DE GOHORT** A knight of the Round Table, he was Perceval's* uncle who taught him the requisites of arms and horses and knighted him. He warned his nephew against talking too much. He was also the uncle of Blancheflor*. In Wolfram he is given three sons and a daughter.

**GOSPEL OF THOMAS** An apocryphal gospel which Phillips thinks was the Grail*. It contains 114 sayings, set to have come from Jesus* to Thomas. It formed part of the Nag Hammadi Library, found in Egypt in 1945. It was written in Coptic. Earlier fragments discovered had been written in Greek. The date of the Gospel is uncertain. In it, Jesus* advises against praying, fasting and giving to the poor, which tends to put it at odds with the canonical gospels. Some of Jesus' utterances are said to be secret sayings. The 114th saying, added to the others, has Peter opposing Mary (?Magdalen) because she is not male, but Jesus says he will make her male. It is said that Mani, the founder of Manichaeism, somewhat of an offshoot of Gnosticism, revered the work.

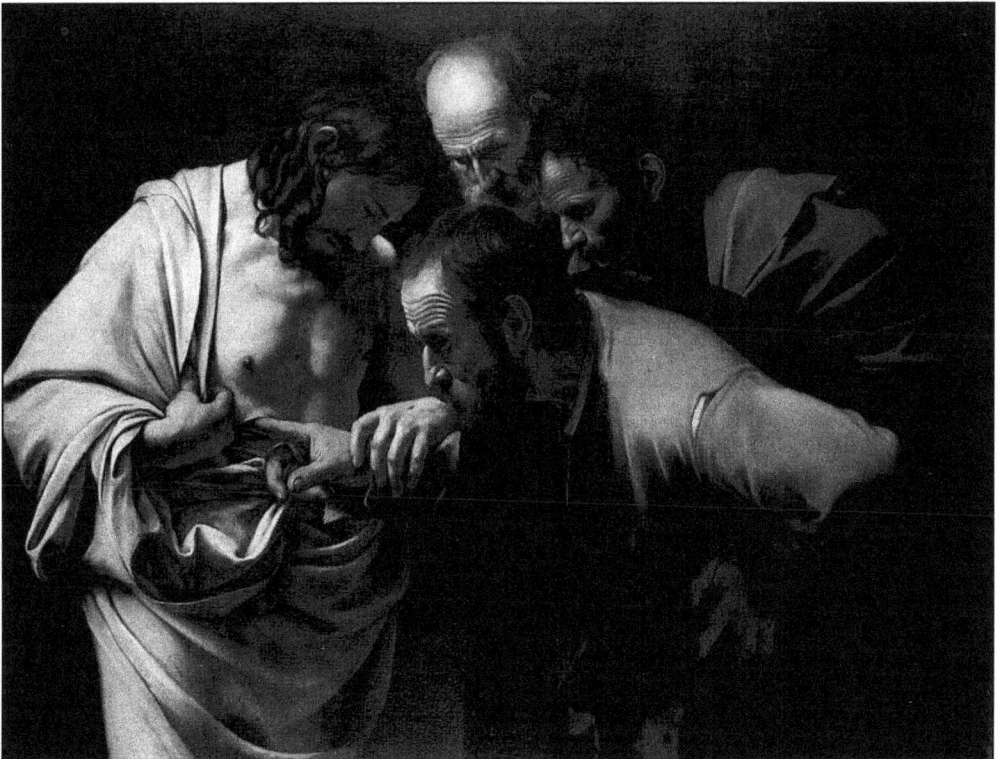

**GOTTINE** A German word signifying a goddess or fairy. In *Diu Crône*, one of these is the Grail* bearer and she ends up ruling the Grail Castle*.

**GRAAL** *see* Grail.

**GRA-AL** According to Nahmad and Bailey, this was a Grail* princess born in ancient times to the King and Queen of Ur (in modern Iraq).

In Akkadian and Sumerian mythology the Annunaki* were the gods and one of their number, Marduk, had defeated the monstrous Tiamat, as recounted in the poem *Enuma Elish*. However, Nahmad and Bailey feel that Tiamat was the true goddess, whom Marduk failed to render extinct by his act. Anu, the chief of the Annunaki, wished Gra-al to marry Marduk, to facilitate an invasion of earth by the Naphidem (an unpleasant bunch). Gra-al, having received powers from Tiamat, fled to Britain, where she married the King of Avalon*. She was hidden in passages in Glastonbury Tor* and had a daughter named Brigid. Gra-al was the first Lady of the Lake. This information seems to be based on the results of attempts to access the Akashic Record*.

**GRAIL**

1. **Meaning:**
The meaning of this word is simple enough - it means a kind of dish. It is found as Provençal/Occitan *grazal* and Catalan *grasal* coming ultimately from Latin *gradalis* (in stages) as food was served in it at each stage of the meal. The Grail itself was brought around between each course. It was clearly a vessel, as we are told it did not hold a pike, a salmon or a lamprey. It just contained the Sacred Host. Wolfram tells us it was a stone, an emerald that dropped from Lucifer's crown. Some people ascribe this to a poor knowledge of French on Wolfram's part. However, it is not impossible that Wolfram used elements from other traditions. Wolfram's stone was large enough to bear an inscription. In Robert, however, we find it described quite clearly as a chalice, the cup of the Last Supper. It is as the Cup of the Last Supper it is generally thought.

2. **Content:**
It is difficult to say to what extent the Grail itself is important and to what extent its content. In Chrétien, the important element is clearly the Sacred Host, which it contains.

The *Second Continuation* says it contained Christ's blood. Wolfram says the Sacred Host was placed on the Grail*, which he conceives to be a stone, on Good Friday, giving it the power to feed the Grail company. However, if its remoter origins are in a sacred cauldron*, the cauldron would seem to be the important element.

In the English *Sir Perceval*, the nearest thing to a Grail is Arthur's cup and there is no doubt that when this is taken from him so too is his vitality and we may safely guess that in the original version, the fecundity of the land suffered.

It is said that in *Peredur* there is no Grail, but a head. However, unless its bearer was carrying it by the hair, we can assume she used a vessel or on a platter or at least something else on which it is convenient to lay decapitated heads. It is, however, the head that is important here. It is used to tell Perceval of his task of vengeance and in the original it may have served an oracular purpose.

The Grail is also said, when held before someone, to supply whatsoever food or drink he desires. Gazing at the Grail retards the ageing process.

### 3    Stone :
In Wolfram we are told the Grail was a stone, not a vessel. Quite where this idea sprang from is a mystery. Some said that Wolfram's French was at fault, but this seems a very simplistic explanation. There are certain oriental elements in Wolfram's saga and he may have used some oriental source. Meteors have in some cultures been regarded as sacred stones from heaven. There may have been such a legend which Wolfram picked up.

### 4    Blood:
John Hardying* (or Harding) suggested the true meaning of *Sangréal* was 'holy blood'. This idea is rendered unlikely by its lateness and also such a notion does not fit in with the story by other authors.

### 5    Fish:
The whole business of the Grail's* connection with the fish of the Fisher King* cannot be explained with certainty. Chrétien's statement that the Grail did not contain a pike, salmon or lamprey may indicate that, in the original story, it did bear fish. For a discussion of this *see* Epilogue.

### 6    Procession:
That the Grail Procession* was not of Christian origin seems highly likely. Someone - Chrétien or perhaps a predecessor - christianised it by making the Host replace whatever was supposedly in it before, but the composition of the Procession seems to obviate a Christian origin. In choosing the Host, Chrétien may have been influenced by the general debate concerning transubstantiation* which was in the air.

### 7    Purpose :
The purpose of the Grail seems to be to restore the health of the King and, through that, the fecundity of the land. In Celtic belief, the health and fecundity of the land was bound up with the King's health and strength. Once the latter started to ebb, the king was originally killed, in all probability, and a younger king installed. Later, a surrogate king was killed while the older King kept out of sight. In the Grail saga, the King has been injured through the thighs (an euphemism for castration) and the Grail Knight's question is necessary to restore his fertility and that of the land round about, which, because of his injury, has become unproductive and desolate. It is not impossible that in the original tale (now lost) the quester was the young king who either slew the old king or was slain himself in the old king's place. For the possible manner of the killing of the surrogate *see* Wasteland. The same sort of idea is found behind the story of the King of the Wood at Lake Nemi in Fraser's *Golden Bough*. The point is reinforced by the claim that when the Grail was placed before someone, he could have any food or drink he desired.

**GRAIL CASTLE**   The castle housing the Grail*, often called Corbenic*. Wolfram calls it Monsalvaesche*. In *Diu Crône* it is named Illes*. We are told in *Perlesvaus* it was surrounded by a river that flowed from the earthly Paradise. It had three names, Eden*, Castle of Joy and Castle of Souls. When there, both Gawain* and Bors* had to undergo ordeals as a test.

In various Arthurian romances there are references to a Castle of the Horn. This may be identical with the Grail Castle, the reference being to horns of plenty.

**GRAIL CHURCH**  In full, the Catholic Apostolic Church of the Holy Grail.  It was founded in 1973 by Sean Manchester.  His title is Bishop of Glastonbury.

**GRAIL COUNTERPART**  According to D. Hughes, the real Grail* was taken to Heaven by Jesus*, where it may be found today.  However, it has a counterpart on earth which is a relic.

The Grail Quest*, avers Hughes, led to King Anfortas, who was brought to Britain* and placed in Dinas Bran*.  Helyas the Swan Knight, the last Grail King*, brought it to Jerusalem at the time of the First Crusade.  Hughes seems to identify the Grail with the Antioch Chalice*.

**GRAIL CROP CIRCLE**  There appeared in Wiltshire in 2010 near Avebury a crop circle in the shape of the Holy Grail*.  Whether a hoax or not, it is certainly impressive.  Photographer Steve Alexander claimed that earlier in the year two circles depicting Christ on the Shroud of Turin* had appeared beside the M4.

**GRAIL FAMILY**  The family from which the Grail Keepers came was delineated as follows by Albrecht in *Der Jungerer Titurel.*

- Sennabor, Prince of Cappadocia had three sons: Parille, Azubar and Sabbilar.
- Parille married Argusilla, daughter of the Emperor Vespasian*.
- Their son Titurisone married Elizabel of Aragon.
- Their son Titurel* married Richonde.
- Titurel was the father of Frimutel* who was the father of Anfortas*, Herzeloyde*, Trevrizent*, Tchoysiane and Urepanse.

**GRAIL FAMILY (KING & BEVERIDGE)**  J. King and J. Beveridge contend the Judaic royal family, descended from King David, still exists and is known  as the Grail Family.  They include Arthur* amongst its members.  From time to time exceptional members of the dynasty appear, including Jesus*.  These are styled Grail Kings and Grail Queens.  They are governed by a Grail Code.  Their blood is to be found in the veins of the majority of European noble families.

**GRAIL FAMILY (MOORE)**  A writer named Maree Moore contends there is a Grail Family who, through the generations, have been hoping to restore the Golden Age of Atlantis.  She says this plan was started  by El Morya and Kuthumi.  These two characters feature in the beliefs of Theosophists and are mentioned by Madame Blavatsky and Miss Moore claims they are Masters who have reincarnated as various prominent persons over the centuries.  The first of these, in earlier works referred to simply as Morya, was supposedly encountered by Blavatsky in London in 1851 and was a Rajput.  Another member of this supposed band is the Comte de Saint Germain, (opposite) who flourished in the 18th Century.

Various legends about him claimed he was immortal, probably enhanced by the stories told about him by an English comedian who impersonated him in Paris.  Amongst Theosophists he is regarded as an Ascended Master.

Maree Moore claims that Kuthumi was incarnated as Leonardo da Vinci*, John Dee, Pythagoras, Aristotle, Saint Patrick, King Arthur* and Omar Khayyam.  El Morya was Abraham and King Solomon.  St Germain was Noah, Christopher Columbus, Francis Bacon, Joseph of Arimathea* and Merlin*.

**GRAIL HALLOWS**  A term sometimes applied to objects seen in the Grail Procession* - cup, lance,

dish and sword. A similarity has been noted with the special artefacts of the Tuatha Dé Danaan* - cauldron, spear, sword and the Stone of Destiny.

**GRAIL KINGS** As the saga of the Grail* progressed, a line of Grail Kings became part of the story. Their castle of Corbenic* was in the land of Listenois, perhaps in the Lake District.

*Line of Grail Kings*

- Joshua*, brother of Alain*, married the daughter of Alfasein*, King of the Strange Country, and was the father of:
- Aminadab*, father of
- Carcelois*, father of
- Manuel*, father of
- Lambor*, father of
- Pellehan*, father of
- Pelles*.

**GRAIL LANCE** The lance borne in the Grail Procession*. It was identified as the lance that pierced the side of Christ on the Cross. A great ululation arises when it appears. It is said it will destroy the land of Logres*, though I suspect it has already done so by wounding the Fisher King* and destroying the fecundity of the country.

There have been relics claiming to be the lance that pierced Christ. St Antoninus of Piacenza claimed to have seen it in Rome in 570. Cassiodorus also says it was in Jerusalem in the 6th Century. One relic claimed to be the lance reached Rome in 1492. Another lance, well-known, sometimes called the Lance of St Maurice, is said to have a nail embedded in it that was one of the ones used in the Crucifixion. The nail may be of the right date, but learned opinion tends to place the manufacture of the spearhead about the 7th Century.

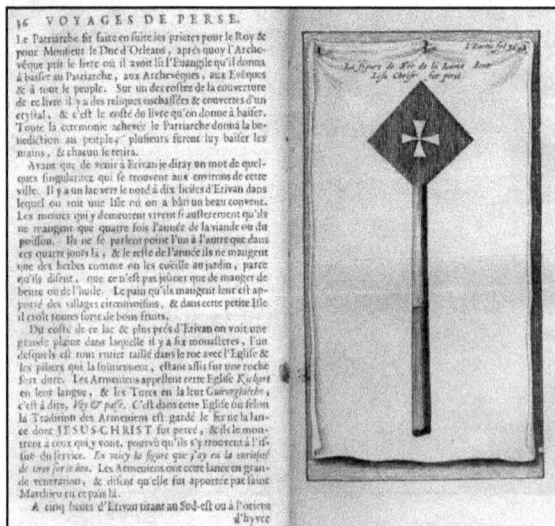

The Lance seen by St Antoninus seems unlikely to have been in a Grail Castle* in the 5th/6th Centuries. Chrétien asserts the lance drips blood while Wolfram merely describes it as bloodstained. A possible Celtic source has been the object of some speculation concerning the weapon. It has been compared with an Irish spear called the *Luin*, which was held over a cauldron of black fluid into which it was plunged whenever it caught fire. This cauldron contained a horrible mixture made by magic from the blood of dogs, cats and druids. (I don't know how the druids felt about this). Its owner, Celtchair, had himself been castrated by a spear wound, in the manner of the Grail King*. An Irish sword, the Crimall, was said to flame and needed blood to stop the fury of its strike. Irish legends could easily have been diffused in Britain* owing to the Irish

dynasty which reigned in Dyfed and the Irish colony in Gwynedd. There were also Irish in the north of Cornwall. However, no Irish spears from legend have been known to actually bleed, nor does it seem that any British ones did so. J.L. Weston favoured an explanation which made the lance a phallic symbol.

There are specific pieces of information regarding the Lance in Grail literature. Chrétien says it was a white lance with a white head. One Continuation identifies the blood with that of Christ. Although the Lance dripped into a vessel, this never overflowed, for it passed through a pipe of green emerald which bore it from the hall.

In Wolfram we are told the Lance was the one which had wounded the Grail King*, but, when the pain grew too severe, it could be inserted in the wound to ease it.

Just what the origin of the Grail* Lance is must remain open to speculation.

To the bearer of the lance at the Crucifixion the name Longinus has been given, but this is a derivative of Greek *longche* (lance).

**GRAIL LINEAGE** According to B. Dunford, this had its origin in the Glenlyon and Fortingall area of Scotland, where the first Christian church was built *before* Jesus' time by druids and persons from the Egyptian mystery schools linked with the Essenes. The ancestors of Jesus, he avers, were brought from Scotland to Galilee.

**GRAIL PROCESSION** This Procession, observed at different times by Perceval* and Gawain*, is variously described:-

(a)    in Chrétien, there was a squire with the Grail Lance*, two squires carrying ten-branched candlesticks, a damsel with the Grail* and a damsel with a tailleor*;

(b)    in the *Didot-Perceval* there was a squire with a lance, a damsel with two silver plates and cloths and a squire with the blood of Christ.

(c)    in *Diu Crône* there were two damsels with lights, two knights with a spear, two damsels with a toblier* and the most beautiful woman in the world with a weeping damsel. The woman took a piece of bread from the box broke it into three parts and gave one piece to the old man.

(d)    in *Perlesvaus* there was a damsel with the Grail*, a damsel with a lance and two angels with candlesticks; the second time the Procession entered the number of damsels and angels seemed to have increased to three of each. There was a Child in the Grail which turned into Christ crucified.

(e)    In *Peredur* a head is borne on a platter. However, it may be argued that the platter is the Grail, the head its contents.

(f)    In the *First Continuation* there is no Procession: the Grail comes in by itself.

(g)    In the *Second Continuation* the Procession consists of Grail, Lance and Broken Sword.

(h)    In the *Third Continuation* the Procession consists of Grail, lance and tailleor.

**GRAIL QUESTION** The Grail Question, which Perceval* should have asked to restore the Fisher King* to health, was "What is the Grail? Whom does it serve?" U.T. Holmes, who feels the story as told by Chrétien was Jewish in content and that Chrétien himself was a converted Jew, thinks the question would have been that of the Passover, "Why is this night different from other nights?" leading to an account of the Exodus. J. Grigsby avers the essential purpose of the question is to promote a dialogue with the Fisher King (or with the disembodied head*) in which ancient lore will be revealed to the interrogator. This head could be induced to communicate and receive information from the primal fish of knowledge, which could reveal the necessary brain mechanism to restore the Golden Age.

**GRAIL TABLE**  Joseph of Arimathea* on his wanderings with his followers was instructed to make a table in the name of the table of the Last Supper.  It became the second of three tables, the third being the Round Table* of King Arthur*.

**GRAIL TEMPLE**  In the *Jungerer Titurel* of Albrecht, an ornate structure  in which the Grail* was housed.  Before it was constructed, the Grail had been floating in the air.  The Temple had a dome.  The roof of the temple itself was of gold, that of the dome studded with sapphires to make it look like the blue sky, while carbuncles marked the stars.  An ornamental sun and moon moved through a zodiac.  The seven canonical hours were marked by the clash of golden cymbals.  Aloe wood was used on the seats. Gold, niello and jewels were on all sides.  The Temple had 22 chapels radiating out from it.

The Persian temple of Taq-i-Taqdis, built in the time of Chosroes II (590-628) in Azerbaijan, may have been the inspiration for the structure.

**GRAUSIN**  In the *Tavola Ritonda*, he was one of Arthur's* knights killed in the Grail* Quest.

**GRINGALAS**  A knight who took part in the Grail* Quest.

**GWAIR**  Mentioned in *Preiddeu Annwn*, we are told that he was chained up in front of the Spoils of Annwn* which Arthur* and his crew were seeking.  He was one of the Three Exalted Prisoners of Britain, the *Triads* inform us.  Just what he did to end up in such a state of incarceration is unknown.  There may have been a tradition he was imprisoned on Lundy, which was called Ynys Wair by the Welsh.  Some of the islands off the coast of Britain were credited with an otherworldly character.

J. Grigsby would identify him with Mabon son of Modron ("Son, son of Mother") who was rescued by Arthur* in *Culhwch ac Olwyn*.  He regards him as being a parallel to the Grail*, his rescue being equivalent to the achievement of the Grail in other sources.  Mabon is in fact the Welsh version of the early British god Maponos, Modron, his mother, being called in Brythonic Matrona.  She was regarded as the goddess of the River Marne and in Arthurian legend became Morgan Le Fay*.

# H

**HAMDON HILL** A hill in Somerset. It was said that monks fleeing from Glastonbury* buried treasure here, including the Grail*. It might be added that, historically, the monks had never claimed to have the Grail.

Hamdon Hill is owned by the Duchy of Cornwall. It is now a country park. There has been much quarrying on the top of the hill.

**HARDYNG, JOHN** (1378-1465; date approximate) English chronicler whose chronicle included Grail* materials. He wrote when of advancing years and the verse in which his chronicle is couched is not prized. He produced his chronicle in two versions, the Long Chronicle, which has yet to see publication, and the Short Chronicle, which, the discerning reader will infer, is shorter than the Long Chronicle. He treated the stories of Joseph of Arimathea* and the Grail* as historical matter, which was unusual amongst chroniclers.

**HAWKSTONE GRAIL** An alabaster cup discovered in Shropshire about 1917.

It has been suggested that Mary Magdalen* collected the blood of Christ in this. The cup is made of onyx and may have been originally a scent jar.

There were a number of local Arthurian tales connected with the area. As early as Camden's era, for example, the Iron Age fort at Bury Camp was said to have been famous in Arthur's time.

One is now told there that Merlin knew the secret of the Grail* and was transformed into an eagle. It is also nowadays claimed that Arthur* is buried in the vicinity. This lore may have developed recently.

**Weaving and Magic**

Where the story began: Christ and his disciples are said to have drunk from the chalice at the Last Supper

# And lo, in an attic near Coventry, the quest for the Grail is ended

By BILL MOULAND

FOR centuries, people have searched for it, made films about it and even claimed it as their own. The Holy Grail — the cup said to have been used by Jesus and his disciples at the Last Supper — has remained elusive.

But now the long quest is over, according to the religious sanctuary, says psychologist Graham Phillips. He points instead to a junk box in the attic of a detached Victorian house near Coventry.

Competition for the honour of tracing the true Holy Grail is fierce — Hello! magazine recently carried a photograph of the Pope venerating the chalice at its supposed home in Spain — so Dr Phillips has produced a book full of lengthy historical detail to back up his own claims.

Far from being the bejewelled artefact depicted by religious painters and the Monty Python comedy

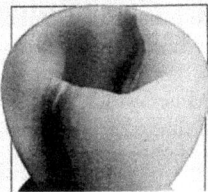

Legendary owner: King Arthur

91

**HAYLING ISLAND** Island on the coast of Hampshire, population 17,000, area 16 square miles/30 square kilometres. V.P. Jones has suggested that it was to this island the Grail* was taken. He suggests that Sinah Common on the island derives from a Celtic *sanctonddcwpan*, 'holy cup'. He goes on to suggest that Higworth means 'Garden of the Holy Grail'. He quotes a tradition that great treasure is said to be buried to the west of St Mary's Church, which was built around 1200. He points out that the spire of this church is tilted towards Higworth and Sinah. He also wonders if the name Hayling means 'Island of the Holy Grail'.

Jones also speculates that the Grail may still repose on the island, perhaps hidden in the stonework of St Mary's Church, perhaps in the rubble of an ancient temple on the island.

**HEAD** There was an important cult of the head amongst the Celts. Carved heads were widespread in Gaul. The taking of heads by Celts is illustrated on Trajan's Column in Rome. Heads of impaled enemies proliferate in Irish literature. A carved head on a pebble from Mecklin Park, Cumbria, is as old as about BC 1400. Bearded heads are to be found on coins issued by the Catuvellani, a tribe to the north of the Thames.

Bran's* expedition to Ireland is probably a prototype of the Grail* quest. Here he was wounded by a poisoned spear in the foot and told his followers to cut off his head. The head remained alive and they brought it with them. On their return they took shelter in a building on the otherworldly island of Gwales, which was sometimes identified as the island of Grassholm. There in the building they feasted for eighty years overseen by the vital head. When Heilyn opened the door, the feast came to an end.

Gardner and Osborn argue that the head may have had to do with a shamanic experience. Arthur went looking for a cauldron* in the Otherworld* in *Preiddeu Annwfn*, but the Otherworld was in one's own subconscious, so therefore one had to enter one's own head, where one discovered it in one's deep psychological reaches. There may have been some sort of actual fane where one underwent preparation for this. Arthur's discovery of the head of Bran may be a way of saying he had the same experience of the god. The human king was supposed to be an archetype of the god. He became the god whose head he finds by his internal experience, the same enlightening experience as the god-king had undergone. Their argument would be that head and Grail were identical.

**HEAD OF CHRIST** K. Laidler believes the Grail* was a codeword for the embalmed head of Christ, revered by the Templars*. He holds it is buried underneath the Apprentice Pillar* at Rosslyn Chapel*.

**HEBRON** A biblical variant of the name Bron*, sometimes used by Robert, who gives the same character both names.

**HECUBA** This is usually considered to be a feminine name, as in Greek mythology it was borne by the wife of King Priam of Troy. However, in Arthurian romance it is the name of a (male) knight who took part in the Grail* Quest.

**HEINRICH VON DEM TURLIN** (13th Century) The author of the German Grail* romance *Diu Crône*, in which Gawain* is the successful Grail quester.

**HELAIN LE BLANC** *see* Elyan the White.

**HELAIUS** The nephew or grandson (*nepos*) of Joseph of Arimathea* according to John of Glastonbury. He was an ancestor of Arthur*, his line of descent being similar to, but not identical with, that of Galahad* in the *Queste*.

**HELINAND OF FROIDMONT** (*Helinandus Frigidimontis*) A Cistercian writer who lived from the 12th to the 13th Centuries. He gave what is considered the basic definition of a grail*: *scutella lata et aliquandtulum profunda* (a broad and, to an extent, deep dish).

**HERMIT KING** Perceval's* uncle, who gave him information about the Grail* and its keepers. He was called Elyas Anais, but was also identified with Pelles*. R.S. Loomis sees a parallel with Crimall, the uncle of the Irish hero Finn mac Cumhaill, who was found by his nephew in the wilderness. There is doubt about which side of the family of the hero he came from.

**HERMOINE** A spirit in the *Estoire* whom Nascien* met at sea. In life he had been from Tarsus and had baptized the wife of Evelake*.

**HERTFORD** Town in England (population 24,000). According to local brothers named Acheson, the Templars* fled there after the destruction of the order in France. They claim there are many tunnels under the town, where information about the Grail* may lie. In St Andrew's Church in the town there is a stained glass window which is said to contain a clue to the nearby whereabouts of the Grail.

**HERZELOYDE** Perceval's* mother in Wolfram. Her father was King Tampenteire. Her first marriage was to a man called Castis, but it was unconsummated. Her second was to Gahmuret*, Perceval's father. She was the Queen of Wales and Northgalis. (The latter simply means *North Wales* and must be ascribed to geographical confusion). Wolfram tells us that in her day the capital of Wales was Kanyolets and that of Northgalis Kingrivals.

**HESUS** Some writers argue that the druids were expecting Christianity because they had a god called Hesus/Esus in their pantheon whose name resembled that of Jesus*. This accounted for the friendly way in which some say they greeted Joseph of Arimathea*. In fact, Hesus had nothing to do with Jesus* - the names are merely similar. (The identification was first made by the unreliable Iolo Morgannwg). We have no evidence that Hesus was ever actually worshipped in Britain, but it is not impossible that he was.

Existing evidence shows him to have been a Gaulish god and Lucan (who may have had an anti-Gaulish bias) says he was a god for whom human sacrifices were hanged from trees and then wounded. He may have been the especial god of a tribe called the Esuvii.

**HIGH HISTORY OF THE HOLY GRAIL**  An alternative title of the *Perlesvaus*.

**HOLY COAT**  The term used for the seamless tunic of Christ, for which the soldiers drew lots. H. Freedman contends this was the original Grail*, pointing out that Aramaic *grl* means a lot in the gambling sense. Two places claim to have the Holy Coat as a relic. One is Trier, where, according to tradition, it was brought by St Helena. People have believed it was there since about 1100. The other is Argenteuil, whither it was traditionally brought by Charlemagne. Its earliest mention is in a document of 1156.

**HOLY VESSEL**  According to V.G. Swanson, there was a vessel of the Grail* so called, but it was merely a symbol of the real Grail, which was a dynasty.

**HORN OF BRAN GALAD**  One of the Thirteen Treasures of the island of Britain. Although the word *galad* signifies a miser, the Horn was given to Merlin*. Presumably a drinking horn, it was suggested it was a prototype for the Grail*. This contention would be strengthened if this Bran could be identified with the Bron* of the Grail legend.

**HUMILDIS**  In *Diu Crône*, a knight who took part in the Grail* Quest.

# I

**ILID** An alternative name for Joseph of Arimathea*, perhaps invented by Iolo Morganwg.

**ILLES** Name of the Grail Castle* in *Diu Crône*.

**INGLIART** Gawain's* war-horse, which originally came from the Grail Castle* of Munsalvaesche*. It later became Perceval's*. It was noted for its short ears.

**INTERMEDIARIUS** A writer of the early 20th Century who expounded on sundry unusual topics, information on which he seems to have claimed to have received by paranormal means. Mentioning the Grail*, he thought only Galahad* achieved it and that Perceval* became Grail King*. His true identity is quite unknown.

**IOLO MORGANWG** This was the bardic name of Edward Williams (1747-1826). He was an antiquarian, but much of the material he produced about early Britain* issued from the wellspring of his imagination and he is not to be trusted as a source for material relevant to the Grail*.

**IRELAND** Where this country is mentioned in *Branwen* and *Culhwch ac Olwen*, it is probably an euhemerisation of the Otherworld*.

**ISAIAS** A knight who went on the Grail* Quest.

**ISLE OF ABUNDANCE** The island where Perceval* landed in *Perlesvaus*. He was told when he returned, he would do so as king, but if he failed in his royal duties he would be consigned to the Isle Suffrotose.

**IVORY HORN** A possible doublet of the Grail* mentioned in the *First Continuation*. It provided food and drink.

A. PIEPERHOFF     *Bayreuther Bühnenfestspiele*     HOFPHOTOGRAPH

Verlag von Carl Giessel, Hoflieferant, Bayreuth

I

**JERUSALEM** It has been suggested that the Grail* has been hidden in the sewers of Jerusalem by Jesus' followers. The system is very complex and would supply a valuable hiding place. A further suggestion is that the disciples hid it there for they knew the Ark of the Covenant* was hidden in the same area.

**JESCHUTÉ** In Wolfram, Perceval* had been told to take a kiss from any woman he encountered. This he did to Jeschuté when he found her sleeping. This caused marital complications for the unfortunate woman, but Perceval reconciled her with her husband. The latter was called Orilus and Perceval had to defeat him in combat to achieve this.

**JESUS CHRIST** He is regarded as an historical figure by most historians. The Bloodline* theory holds that the Grail* was a bloodline descended from Christ and Mary Magdalen*. In the four gospels ascribed to Matthew, Mark, Luke and John (1st Century) there is no indication of a marital or sexual relationship between the two. The later apocryphal gospels, rejected by the Church, have been interpreted as suggesting they had a close relationship, but again there is no direct indication of a sexual union. Moreover, the lateness of these gospels renders them unreliable.

Some have argued that Jesus must have been married, because he was a rabbi. However, in those far off days the regulations regarding the rabbinate were not so strict and it is also possible that, when he was addressed as rabbi, this was a courtesy title.

Margaret Starbird has argued that Jesus was the father of the gypsy Sarah*. For further information *see* Mary Magdalen, Sarah.

According to L. Gardner, Jesus' ascension was when he became a priest. He became a priest king or Fisher King* in the monastery and his male line descended through the Fisher Kings.

The idea that Jesus accompanied Joseph of Arimathea* to Britain* has been put forward by a number of writers. He is supposed to have dedicated the church at Glastonbury*, but this involves post-Resurrection appearances in the accounts as they now stand. We were told by C.V.P. Day, Vicar of Glastonbury in 1920, that there was a legend that Jesus had come to Glastonbury and that the Grail was buried on Chalice Hill. In Webb's *Glastonbury Ynyswitrin* (1929) we are informed of a tradition that Jesus came as a boy to Priddy, a Somerset village, underneath which lies a tunnel called Swilden's Hole. There was a saying in the vicinity, "As sure as Our Lord came to Priddy". According to Mary Caine, there is a tradition he stayed at the New Inn there. H.A. Lewis *Ab Antiquo* (1935) quotes an aged Mrs George of Polperro (Cornwall) who had heard that Cornwall had been visited by Jesus. There is a Jesus

Well near Padstow in Cornwall, which has been cited as evidence of Jesus' visit. He is said to have landed at Place, Fowey, St Just in Roseland and Looe Island. At St Day there was a saying that Jesus visited the mines. According to Mary Caine, it was because of the Glastonbury Zodiac*, the Grail story etched out in the landscape, that Jesus came to Britain in the first place.

**JOHN MARTINUS** According to allegedly channelled material from Thoth (an ancient Egyptian god) through Maia and Simeon Nartoomid, Jesus* and Mary Magdalen* had a son named John Martinus, perhaps born on Iona. He was conceived after Jesus rose from the dead.

John Martinus went to Ephesus with Mary Magdalen, where she died. He ultimately brought the Grail* to Glastonbury*.

John Martinus married Elizabeth and they had a daughter named Sara. Elizabeth died. He subsequently married Muriel. They had two sons, Thomas and Germane. Sara had a daughter named Sara Berenice.

**JOHN** According to L. Hake *Something new on men and manners* (1828) we are told that John, a bishop, was the son of Joseph of Arimathea*. They arrived in Britain with ten others.

**JOHN OF GLASTONBURY** (1393-1464) A chronicler who produced a work called *Cronica sive Antiquitates Glastoniensis Ecclesiae*. In this work he claimed Joseph of Arimathea had brought two cruets containing the blood and sweat of Christ to Glastonbury. He did not mention the Grail* itself.

**JOSEPH OF ARIMATHEA** After Christ's resurrection, he was imprisoned in Jerusalem, according to Grail* romance. Where exactly Arimathea was is uncertain, perhaps modern Rentis. Robert says in his poem about Joseph that he had the Grail, which is for the first time referred to as the cup of the Last Supper. He later caught some blood of Christ in it.

Joseph was imprisoned, where he was visited by Christ, who gave him the cup.

Free at last, he set off with a group of followers and was told to build a table like that of the Last Supper. An empty place, symbolising Judas, was to be left at the table. Joseph sent Bron and Peter to the west.

In the *Estoire* Joseph actually went to Britain itself and had various adventures there (*see* Crudel, Camelot). He had been rescued from prison after Jerusalem was captured by Vespasian* in AD 70. A late romance brought him as far as Norway.

An interpolation found in certain manuscripts of the *First Continuation* informs us he made the Grail* himself and in it he caught blood flowing from the crucified Christ. He locked the Grail in a wardrobe between which two candles burned. He was imprisoned in a tower, but escaped. He and Nicodemus* set off in a ship and came to the White Isle (? the Isle of Wight) which was partially owned by England. They made a

S. JOSEPH OF ARIMATHEA

settlement and were left unmolested for two years. After that there was fighting with locals, followed by a famine. Joseph asked for the Grail*, which appeared and fed all.

In his work on Glastonbury*, William* of Malmesbury does not mention Joseph* but said the Old Church there was the oldest known in England. The floor was inlaid with polished stones. In the paving were stones laid by design in triangles and squares lined with lead. He said that if he believed some holy secret reposed beneath it, he did no injustice to religion. A later writer (late 13th Century) added to the work that Joseph and his son Josephes* came to England. The abbey developed a tradition that Joseph arrived in 63 AD. He is mentioned in a strange Latin prophecy ascribed to a man named Melkin*. John the Apostle entrusted Mary the Virgin to Joseph, according to John of Glastonbury, who also claimed Joseph had brought two cruets to Britain containing the blood and sweat of Christ. In Pynson's *Lyfe of Joseph of Arimathea* (1520) it is said that blood from Jesus'* wound adhered to Joseph's chest and was placed in two cruets. Pynson is the first to mention the Holy Thorn* of Glastonbury.

Medieval genealogies made Joseph the uncle of Mary or of her husband, Joseph. C.W. Bennet (1845-1935) said there was an Irish legend that Joseph was the uncle of Jesus, but I have never seen an Irish source for this.

Rabanus Maurus (766-856) says Joseph went to Britain. Caesar Baronius, writing about 1500, claimed that when Mary Magdalen* and others had been put in an oarless boat and set adrift, they had taken Joseph with them. They reached Marseilles. Joseph then went to Britain to preach. The *Acta Sanctorum* of the Bollandists mention a tradition that Joseph was sent to Britain by St Philip or St Peter.

B. Lawrence *Somerset Legends* (1973) quotes a tale that says when Joseph reached Glastonbury he was told by the angel Gabriel to build a church in honour of the Virgin Mary*. He saw Christ descend and consecrate it.

As to where Joseph was supposedly buried, William Good (1527-86) says the monks were uncertain of his burial place: it was either hidden at Glastonbury or at Hamden Hill near Montacute. John of Glastonbury quotes Melkin* as saying he was buried in the abbey. It seems the monks planned to announce that the bodies of Joseph and his followers had been discovered in 1419, but the scheme was aborted. At Glastonbury itself, there had been a subterranean chapel with a statue of the saint. A tomb in the churchyard of the Anglican Church was marked J.A. It was subsequently taken into the church. It had no contents. Some believe it was the tomb of one John Allen. Some suspect it was Joseph's tomb. Tomb in this account seems to mean coffin.

In the *Estoire* Joseph was buried in the Abbey of the Cross in Scotland.

Cressy in his *Church History of Brittany* (1668) says Joseph and his son, named after him, came to Britain towards the end of Nero's reign. He also avers Saints Peter and Paul visited Britain. Another writer, Nicephorus, adds Simon Zelotes to the list of apostolic visitors. H. Rowlands *Mona Antiqua Restorata* (1723) seems pretty sure St Paul preached in Britain and he suggests the country was also visited by James son of Zebedee. That both Joseph and St Paul came to Britain is contended by R.W. Morgan *St Paul in Britain* (1861). This curious Welshman was a clergyman in the Church of England who also ran a denomination of his own founding, the Ancient British Church, calling himself Patriarch Pelagius I.

A late tradition says that Joseph's body was brought from Jerusalem to France.

F.G. Holweck (1856-1927) mentions a daughter of Joseph called St Josa, but provides no biographical information.

L. Gardner's Bloodline* argument identifies Joseph with James the Just and claims he brought Jesus Justus, son of Jesus* of Nazareth, to Britain. Henry Jenner (1848-1934) heard the proverb *Joseph was in the tin trade* in Cornwall. This has led to some speculating that Joseph was a tin merchant, who had been to Britain a number of times.

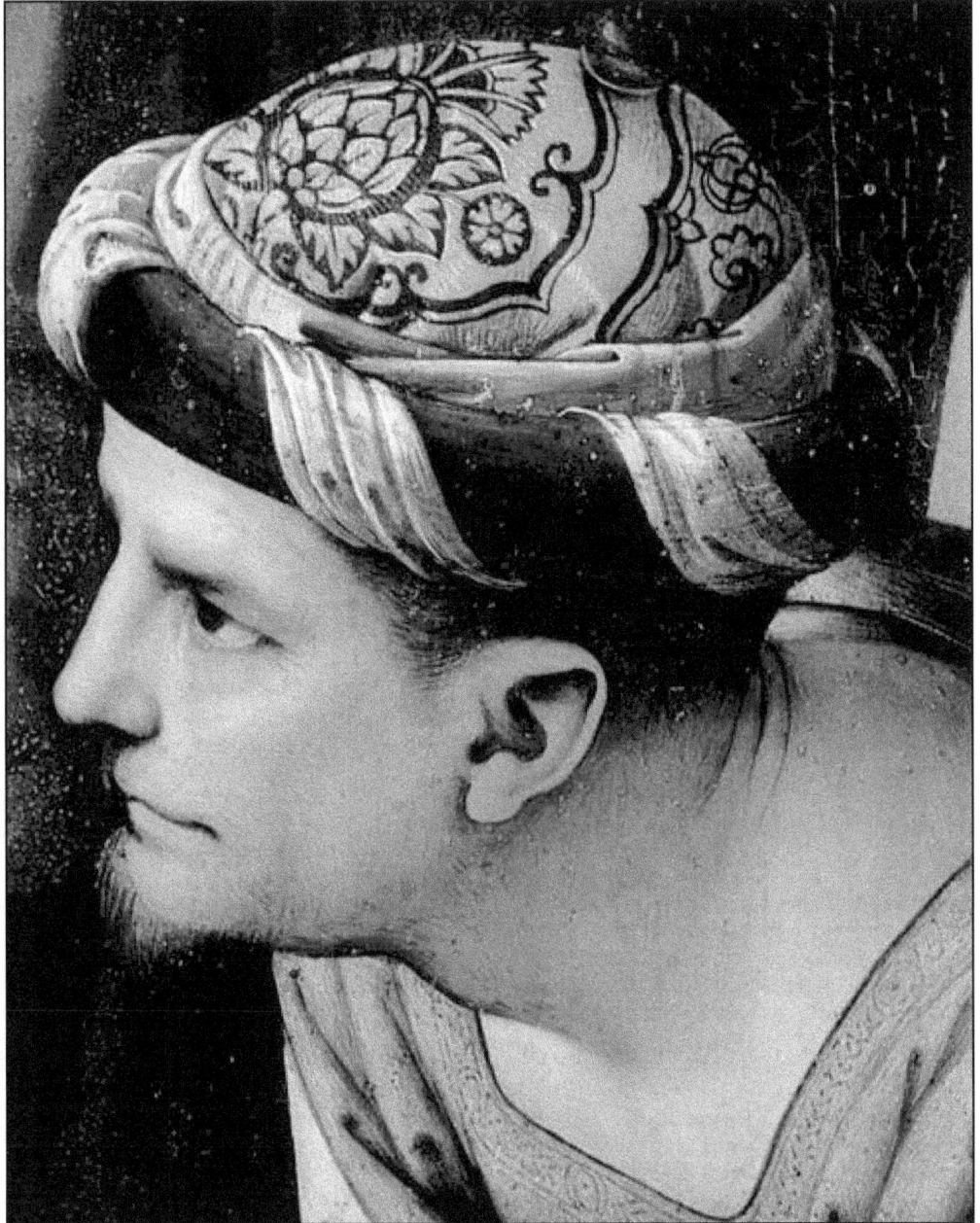

J. Benjamin has mooted the theory that Joseph was the Virgin Mary's father, but this is because he believes the name Joseph to be identical with the name *Joachim*, given to her father in the apocryphal Protoevengelium of James. In fact, the two names are distinct.

A work called *The History of That Holy Disciple Joseph of Arimathea*, perhaps published about 1770, asserts that his father was called Matthias, that he was one of the 72 disciples, that he was sent to Britain, that he died at the age of 86 and that his grave was in the chancel of Glastonbury* Abbey. The Urantia Book, a sort of bible published by the Urantia Foundation in 1955 and of uncertain authorship, claims that two daughters of Joseph were Mary Magdalen* and Rebecca. The website www.biblesearchers.com claims his mother was called Rachel.

Perhaps in the Middle Ages the idea was first mooted that Joseph was the uncle of either the Virgin Mary or St Joseph. The Petragrail website avers that he was the Virgin Mary's twin brother. Bearing in mind that Joseph asked Pontius Pilate for the body of Jesus*, it is not impossible that he and Jesus were related.

**JOSEPH THE COPT**  M. Murray suggested Joseph of Arimathea* did not come to Britain, but another Joseph, a Copt, did in the $3^{rd}/4^{th}$ Century, giving rise to the legend. She feels he may have come from the monastery of Baramus in Egypt.

**JOSEPHES**  The son of Joseph of Arimathea*. When Joseph set out with the Grail*, he went into the ark which contained it where Christ made him a bishop. When his father had preached in the city of Sarras*, many people fell ill because they had refused to convert. Josephe tried to flee the city and was struck in the thigh by a lance. This was removed by an angel and drops of blood from it cured Nascien's* eyes. The latter had become blind from looking at the Grail*.

When Joseph* and his followers finally reached the sea opposite Britain, some were able to cross to it on Josephe's shirt. Those whose faith was weaker had to wait until later, when Nascien* brought them across.

Josephes had sundry adventures in Britain (*see* Crudel, Camelot).  Before dying he went to the abbey where Mordrain* was. He placed a cross on Mordrain's shield made from his own blood. He died the next day. When dying he handed the Grail over to Alan*. After death, his body was taken to Scotland. This replenished the land, which had been struck by famine. He was buried in the abbey of Glays. The name *Josephes* is merely a form of *Josephus*, the Latin form of *Joseph.*

The story that Josephes was made a bishop by Jesus is unusual, because of its impact on the doctrine of the Apostolic Succession. This said that, at the Last Supper, Christ had given the apostles the power to transform the bread and wine into his body and blood. Others who could do it had to be granted the power by any of the apostles, not only Peter.  However, it is not actually impossible that Jesus could have given the power directly to others and they could pass it on, but there is no record of his doing so. Apostolic succession relates to the episcopate, but not to the primacy of the Church. Some writers, who

are shaky on the subject of theology, think that a church founded before Rome would take precedence over Peter's* church. This is not, however, the case. Peter, according to the Bible, was the leading apostle from the outset, wherever he happened to be and before he went to Rome.

L. Gardner asserts Josephes was the son of Christ and Mary Magdalene*.

**JOSEUS** The son of Pelles* in *Perlesvaus*. We are told he killed his own mother. The castle where the matricide occurred burned and will continue to do so, ultimately starting the fire which will end the world. Joseus himself ended up as the custodian of the Grail Castle*.

**JOYCE, DONOVAN (1910-1980)** This Australian writer anticipated the idea that Jesus* was married as entertained by the Bloodline* advocates. He maintained that Jesus survived the Crucifixion, married Mary Magdalen*, had a son and died at Masada aged eighty.

**JULIAN** A knight who went on the Grail* Quest.

Joseph of Arimathea Conversing the Britons.

# K

**KARLSTEIN CASTLE**   A castle in the Czech Republic.  It was built by King Charles of Bohemia (reigned 1346-78).  It includes a tower with, at the top, the Chapel of the Holy Blood, known locally as the Chapel of the Holy Grail\*.  It is said that at on Good Friday the King would go up there to contemplate a crystal cup, which he identified as the Grail.

**KESWICK**  Town in Cumbria (population 5000).  It has been said to have been the site of the Grail Castle*.

**KING OF THE CASTLE MORTAL**  In *Perlesvaus* this unpleasant individual killed the Fisher King* and held the Grail Castle*.  Perceval*  with a mule and a banner provided by King Pelles*, overcame twenty-seven of the King's knights and the King killed himself by throwing himself from the battlements.

**KIUSCHE**  Purity of heart, a quality of several characters in Wolfram.

**KJÖLUR MOUNTAIN PASS**  At this locale in Iceland it was felt by G. Gianazza and T. Thórasson, as a result of uncovering clues, that the Grail* reposed  in an underground chamber.  The chamber seems to have been discovered, but it was filled with water.

**KLINGSOR**  The spelling (taken from Wagner, as it is more familiar) of Clinschor, who makes his appearance in Wolfram.  He lived in Terre de Labur, situated in Italy.  He kept various prisoners, including Arnive, which is the name given to Arthur's* mother in *Parsifal*, as prisoners.  Gawain* rescued them. Klingsor had learned magic in the city of Persida in Persia.  Magic had been invented in this city.  His own capital was the city of Capua in Italy.  In Wagner's *Parzifal* Klingsor has a greater part to play as Perceval's* opponent.

**KOLBRIN BIBLE**  A work which purports to have been written partially by Egyptians and partially by Celts.  It is claimed it was for a time in Glastonbury* Abbey.  However, it only appeared in public in 1992.   In it we are told that Joseph of Arimathea* looked after the Virgin Mary and that was why he came to be called Keeper of the Sacred Vessel.

**KNIGHT IN A BARREL**  In *Perlesvaus* on the Isle of Abundance*, was a barrel, apparently made of glass, containing a knight.  Perceval* tried to speak to him, but he did not reply, nor would the islanders divulge anything about him.

**KNIGHTS OF THE HOLY GRAIL**  A modern Christian order, apparently with headquarters in Bar Harbor (Maine).

**KRATER**  A receptacle for wine used in ancient Greece.  In occultism it was supposed to be a large vessel containing gnosis.  It had been specially sent down to earth.  H.R. and R. Kahane have argued that the Grail* in Wolfram is one of these kraters.  The fact that Wolfram says it is a stone is only a metaphor.

**KUKUMERLAND**  According to Wolfram, the Red Knight* slain by Perceval was named Ither and ruled this country.   Its name means 'cucumber land' and is almost certainly taken from Gurktal (=Cucumber Vale) in Austria.

**KUNDRY**  In Wolfram, the woman who chided Perceval* for not asking the Grail Question*.  She came from a race of people with faces like boars, who lived in the land of Tribalibot, near the Ganges.  She was very learned.  She spoke all languages.  It is after Kundry turns up that the Grail* Quest starts.  Her brother was called Malcreature.  There is another Kundry in the poem, who is Arthur's niece.

**KYOT**  Wolfram claims he was the source of his Grail* epic, but this is widely disbelieved.  It has been suggested he was identical with a troubadour called Guiot of Provins, but we have no narrative poems claiming him as an author.  J. Markale suggests his name may have come from Old French *guille* (guile). W. Hasty *A Companion to Wolfram's Parzival* (1999) says it is accepted by a large body of commentators that Kyot was not a real person.

# L

**LABEL**  A king of Persia in the *Estoire*.  He was on his way to avenge his brother's death when Nascien* converted him to Christianity.

**LAMBOR**  A Grail King*.  In a variant of the Dolorous Stroke* theme, we are told he was fighting King Varlan*, who struck him, causing the land to become a wasteland.  According to Laurence Gardner's Bloodline* hypothesis, *Lambord* was the father of Pellam* and grandfather of Perceval*.  He also claims Lambord was the father of Taliesin*, who married the first Viviane*.

**LANCELOT**  Perhaps the most famous Knight of the Round Table, he is may be best remembered for his intrigue with Guinevere, Arthur's wife.

He took part in the Grail Quest and came to Corbenic*, which had two lions on guard, but, when he drew his sword to fight, his arm was struck by a fiery hand.

He came to a door within the castle, but it would not yield to his attempts to open it.  He felt sure the Grail* lay behind it.  After praying, he was able to open the door and he saw the Grail.  He saw a priest saying Mass and Three Persons, two of them lowering the youngest in the priest's hands. Lancelot went to aid the priest, but was  overcome by the heat and felt hands lifting him out of the room.  He remained senseless for twenty-four days.  When he came to, he was told his quest was over.

There are in fact two accounts of the career of Lancelot.  One involves his affair with Guinevere, but the other, found in the *Lanzelet* romance of Ulrich von Zatzikhoven, knows nothing of such an affair and has him marrying Iblis and their having four children.  What both sources have in common is that he was raised by a fairy in fairyland.  This in fact seems to be the nub of the story.  The present writer suspects that his affair with Guinevere was a later addition, modelled on the story of Tristan. Ulrich's story is almost certainly Celtic in origin, for it features Mabuz, who is almost certainly the Celtic god Mabon.  According to Ulrich, Mabuz was the son of the fairy who brought up Lancelot.  If Mabuz was

Sir Launcelot

indeed Mabon, a name meaning "son", then, according to Celtic mythology his mother was Modron, who was the prototype of Morgan LeFay*.

R.S. Loomis speculates he was identical with a character called Llwch Lleminawch, mentioned in the Welsh poem *Preiddeu Annfwn\**, which is thought a prototype of the Grail Quest and with *Llenlleawch* in the story of Diwrnach*, which is regarded as a somewhat demythologised version of the same story. He reckons these rather lengthy Welsh names were simplified by continental writers by giving him a name similar to Breton *Lancelyn*.

**LANCELOT-GRAIL** (13th Century) A cycle of tales involving the *Estoire de Saint Graal, Prose Lancelot, Queste de Saint Graal, Vulgate Merlin* and *Mort Artu*. It was formerly referred to as the *Vulgate Version*.

**LAPIS EXILIS** In Latin "Exile Stone". This was the name given to the Grail* by Wolfram. Albrecht called it *iaspis et silis*, 'jasper and flint'. It has also been suggested that it is derived from *lapis e coelis*, 'stone from heaven'. It could also be the Philosopher's Stone (*lapis elixir*).

**LEONARDO DA VINCI (1452-1519)** Although generally in the public mind Leonardo is thought of as a painter and sculptor, he was many other things beside. He was a mathematician, musician, architect, town planner, anatomist, scientist and the inventor of prototypes of the helicopter, submarine, diving suit and glider. The earlier part of his life was spent in Italy, the latter in France. His love of the natural world seems to owe much to his rustic childhood. He was a vegetarian and would buy and release caged birds. He regarded war and any infliction of pain with horror and, though he designed weapons, he did so with a view to the defence of liberty. In sum, the man was a genius and seems to have been in many respects a very good man.

Leonardo was not a grand master of the Priory of Sion* as this was a modern invention and has been exposed as a hoax. However, we must still look at his painting *The Last Supper* to see if there is anything regarding a Grail* bloodline* in it, even if such an idea took shape only in the Renaissance. The painting is a mural, i.e., a painting done directly on a wall, rather than a fresco, which would have been executed on plaster. It was painted over the period 1495-8. Each of the apostles in the picture can be identified by name, as a result of an entry in a notebook. The painting has been the object of a restoration project which lasted from 1978-99.

The idea has been put forward that the Apostle John is not who he is supposed to be, but Mary Magdalen*, who, as Christ's wife, would carry on the Bloodline* that would be in fact the Grail*. The painting of John does look somewhat effeminate, but it was part of the artistic tradition of the day to so paint young men.

To the argument that Leonardo did not adhere to the tradition, one can say that the painting of *John the Baptist* (painted 1513-1516), generally supposed to be his, makes the Baptist very effeminate, while another sketch for a painting of the Baptist also shows androgynous characteristics and was later painted over and changed into Bacchus. Both paintings are currently in the Louvre.

The painting is supposed to show the apostles' reaction when Jesus says one of them will betray him. If the figure of John is truly Mary Magdalen, the question arises about the whereabouts of John. The idea that there was a secret belief in the Bloodline of the Grail

and that Leonardo was privy to it is difficult to sustain. There is no evidence for such a tradition stretching back to apostolic times. Even if some later tradition to which Leonardo adhered grew up about Jesus and Mary Magdalene and was current in the Renaissance, there is no evidence for its existence.

**LEWIS, LIONEL SMITTET (1867-1953)** Vicar of Glastonbury. He wrote on the subject of Joseph of Arimathea*, but was uncritical in his approach. A kindly man, he started his work in the East End of London, where he helped the poor and was kind to animals. He was opposed to the views of Dean Armitage Robinson, who had written on Glastonbury.

**LIBERAL CATHOLIC CHURCH GRAIL COMMUNITY** A part of the Liberal Catholic Church (founded 1916), which has split into a number of sections. The Grail Community became an independent Church under Roy Bannister in 1982.

**LILITH** A demoness in Jewish legend. She was Adam's first wife, but abandoned him. In Gardner's Bloodline* she is listed as the mother of Cain's* wife.

**LINCOLN** When the coffin of Bishop Sutton of Lincoln was discovered in the cathedral, a chalice was found with it. Bishop Sutton had been consecrated in 1280. E.C. Coleman has conjectured that this chalice might be the Grail*. He suggests it could have been found in Antioch, which might have been visited by Eleanor of Aquitaine in an unrecorded visit where she was possibly given it. It may then have come into the hands of the Templars* who may have entrusted it to the bishop.

As may be seen, there is much speculation here. R.M.T. Hall dated the chalice to the 13$^{th}$ Century. This is not regarded by Coleman as the final word on the matter.

**LINCOLN, HENRY** (born 1930) Professional name of Henry Soskin whose *Chronicle* programmes on the BBC (1972-9) were followed by the book *The Holy Blood and the Holy Grail* (1982), almost universally dismissed by historians, which he wrote with Michael Baigent and Richard Leigh. This sought to prove the Grail* was the Bloodline* of Jesus Christ.

**LIONEL** The brother of Bors*, he was one of those who went on the quest for the Grail*. When Bors chose to save a damsel in distress when Lionel was under attack, he was somewhat miffed, but in due course the brothers were reconciled.

**LISTENOIS** This was the country of King Calafes, who was converted to Christianity, taking the name Alfasein. It contained the Grail castle of Corbenic*. When Balin* struck the Dolorous Stroke*, it became the Wasteland*. Listenois is perhaps to be identified with Llystin (Dyfed). It may also come from Franco-Welsh *Llys-yn-Nord* which would indicate it was in the north of England. The *Tavola Ritonda* tells us there was a fortress here called Gitedrano.

**LLYN Y PEIR** (=Lake of the Cauldron*) Bran's* cauldron, which features in *Branwen*, had its origin in Ireland*. The cauldron itself may be a prototype of the Grail* and Ireland* here may be a substitution for the Otherworld*. A huge man emerged from Llyn y Peir. His name was Llasar Llaw Gyfnewid. With him came his wife, twice as big as he, called Cymidei Cymeinfoll. The pair of them and their off-spring proved to be destructive, so they were all lured into an iron house, which was made unbearably hot. Their children, who had been born grown warriors, perished, but the parents escaped to Britain*, where they gave the cauldron to Bran.

**LOATHLY DAMSEL** The damsel who, after Perceval* failed to ask the Grail Question*, came and upbraided him for not doing so. She is usually unnamed, but Wolfram calls her Kundry*. Chrétien tells us she had eyes like rats', long ears and a beard and rode on a yellow mule. In the *Perlesvaus* she is bald and has the head of a king in her hand, sealed with silver and crowned with gold. She was accompanied in that work by a second damsel with the head of a queen, sealed with lead and crowned with copper. A third damsel drove the others with a whip. The Loathly Damsel turned out to be the damsel who had borne the Grail. After Perceval captured the Grail Castle* from the King of Castle Mortal*, her hair re-grew.

She may have been in origin a goddess. Heinrich actually calls her one.

**LOGRES** The term for England used in Grail* romances. It was latinised as *Loegria* and ultimately comes from Welsh *Lloegyr*, whose origin is uncertain. It may mean 'near the border'.

**LOHENGRIN** This is the more familiar form of this knight's name from Wagner's opera. He is called *Loherangrin* by Wolfram and *Lohengrin* in a romance called *Rigomer*. The son of Perceval*, he was sent from the Grail Castle* to rescue Elsa of Brabant from an unwanted suitor. He arrived in a boat drawn by a swan. He then married her, but forbade her to ask his name. When she broke this taboo, he

left. He later married Princess Belaye of Lizaborye and was murdered.

He is called *Lorengel* in another German romance, where he did not have to leave Elsa.

**LORGAIREACHT AN tSOIDHIGH NAOMHTHA**  Irish language version of the Grail* Quest.  It perhaps dates from the 15th Century.

**LOVELICH, HENRY** (15th Century) He wrote *The History of the Holy Grail.*  It has been argued that his name should actually be read as Lonelich.

**LUCAN**  A companion of Joseph of Arimathea* in the *Estoire.*  Another Lucan was a philosopher whom God struck dead in the same work.

**LUCIUS** According to Bede, a British king who sent Pope Eleutherius a letter asking to be made Christian. Bede's information comes from the *Liber Pontificalis.*  It is widely accepted that the entry in the latter work is a mistake due to confusion with Abgar VIII, King of Osroene (reigned 177-212), one of whose names was Lucius and whose dwelling was called Britio Edessorum, the Citadel of Edessa.  This idea was put forward by A. von Harnack in 1908.  This theory is doubted, however, by H.M. Porter, who feels Abgar would have approached the much nearer Patriarch of Antioch.  Around that time the patriarchs were Theophilus (169-77) and Maximinus (177-191).  A recent work *King Lucius of Britain* (2008) by D.J. Knight, questions the theory.

Gardner is sure that Lucius was a Briton and places him in his Grail* Bloodline*.  He says that Lucius was a descendant of Joseph of Arimathea* and that his daughter Eurgen married Aminadab*, a descendant of Jesus and Mary Magdalen*.

Neither Geoffrey of Monmouth nor the Book of Llandaff seems to know any earlier tradition of a conversion of Britain.

**LULUWA**  According to Gardner's Bloodline* theory, Luluwa was the wife of Cain*.  Gardner may have obtained the name from the Second Book of Adam and Eve, where it appears.  There were other accounts which claimed different names for Cain's wife, however, such as 'Awan, Balbira and Kalmara. Gardner claims Luluwa was the daughter of Lilith*.

**MADAM** A knight who went on the Grail* Quest. The idea of addressing him as *Sir Madam* cannot but make us smile.

**MAELGWYN** King of Gwynedd in the 6th Century. A. Jackson thinks him identical with the Fisher King*. While mainstream history places Maelgwyn's death in 547, Jackson contends he lived about a century earlier.

**MAIDAROS** A knight who went on the Grail* Quest.

**MAIMED KING** *see* Fisher King

**MAJI (INDIGO/EIEYANI) GRAIL LINES** Lines in whose existence the esoteric order known as the Melchizedek Cloister Emerald Order believe. They claim to base their teachings on discs kept by a family called Eieyani, a line of indigo children, in existence since BC 9558. That "indigo children" classified as children with special paranormal powers exist is not regarded as proven by mainstream psychology.

**MALORY, THOMAS** An English writer of the 15th Century, he wrote what many regard as the standard English version of the Arthurian legends, *Le Morte d'Arthur.* The title given it by the author was *The Whole Book of King Arthur and his Knights of the Round Table,* but when the book was printed by Caxton in 1485 it was under the title by which it is now known. We cannot say anything certain about the author, as it is not certain who, amongst several contemporaries of his name, wrote the book.

**MALTA** Church in Listenois*, perhaps to be identified with Mold in the north of Wales.

**MANATHES** A companion of Joseph of Arimathea* in the *Estoire.*

**MANATUR** Brother of Tholomer* in the *Estoire.* He was killed by Nascien*.

**MANDIN** A knight who went on the Grail* Quest.

**MANDRAKE** Mandrake was well known as an anaesthetic in ancient times and G. Moss has argued that, if Chrétien had finished his Grail* romance, the Grail would have been revealed as a mandrake. She contends Chrétien was advocating a theory whereby Jesus* did not die on the cross, but was given mandrake and vinegar to make him appear dead.

In the 1890s experiments showed that animals to which a dose of mixed alcohol and mandrake was administered stopped breathing but their hearts continued to beat.

However, this does not mean the idea occurred to Chrétien or that such a subterfuge was used at the time of Jesus*.

**MANESSIER** The author of the *Third Continuation* of Chrétien's *Perceval*. We know nothing else about him.

**MANNA MACHINE** G. Sassoon and R. Dale claimed the manna, which fed the wandering Israelites in the Bible, was produced by a nuclear-driven machine, perhaps of extraterrestrial origin. This was kept in the Ark of the Covenant*. The fate of the Ark is a mystery. They base their argument on the Zohar, a qabbalistic book. This is said to date from ancient times (post 70 AD), but it was first produced by Moses de Leon (died 1305), who may have written it. J. and P. Fiebag suggest the device surfaced in Europe as the Grail*. The food producing properties of both items seem to be a reason for the identification.

However, manna is not represented as coming from a machine and may be the product of the tree *Tamarix mamifera*. The word may simply come from Egyptian *mennu*, 'food'.

**MANUEL/MANAAL** A Grail King*, father of Lambor*.

**MARIUS** The successor of Arviragus*, according to Geoffrey. Elsewhere it is said he too gave land to Joseph of Arimathea*.

**MARY MAGDALEN** The idea that Jesus* was married to Mary Magdalen and their descendants were the Bloodline* that was the true Grail* has surfaced in modern times. Material from apocryphal gospels has been adduced in support of this.

The canonical gospels tell us something of Mary Magdalen. Her name indicates she came from Magdala, on the west coast of the Sea of Galilee. She had demons expelled from her by Jesus. She was present at the Crucifixion and saw Jesus after he had risen. The four canonical gospels were penned by roughly 100 AD. Bishop Robinson has argued they were all available by 70 AD.

In Luke 7:37-38 a repentant sinner anoints Jesus. In John there is a similar anointing by Mary of Bethany. In the Western Church it came to be accepted that Mary Magdalen and Mary of Bethany were identical. This led Pope Gregory in a sermon delivered in 591 to identify Mary Magdalen with the sinner. The sermon was on forgiveness: the Pope may have been wrong in identifying the two, as there is nothing in the Bible to suggest the two Marys were the same. However, advocates of the Bloodline* argument say the Pope was trying deliberately to vilify Mary Magdalen as a progenitor of the Bloodline which was seen as a threat to papal power.

From the apocryphal works, notably those found in the Nag Hammadi Library, texts are cited which are said to imply a marital or close relationship between Jesus and Mary Magdalen. The Gospel of Mary ($2^{nd}/3^{rd}$ Century AD) it is said that Jesus loved Mary more than other women; in the Gospel of Thomas ($2^{nd}/3^{rd}$ Century) Jesus said he would make Mary into a male so she would be equal to the apostles; and in the Gospel of Philip, Jesus is said to have kissed Mary often. The surviving document is full of holes and one such hole is at the place which tells us where Jesus placed the kisses. Bloodline advocates have inferred the word 'mouth', but it is by no means certain they are correct.

Moreover, in Gnosticism - and all these books are Gnostic - kissing on the mouth was a means of passing on gnosis, esoteric knowledge. These books were written a long time after those gospels which found their way into the New Testament.

In the Middle Ages one Jacobus de Voraigne produced the *Legenda Aurea*, a collection of saints' lives. He identifies Mary Magdalen with Mary of Bethany and says that with her sister, Martha, her brother, Lazarus and a man called Maximin they were placed in a boat without a rudder or sail and set adrift in the Mediterranean by persecutors. They ended up in Marseilles. Later Mary became an anchoress for 30 years. A variant tradition was that she landed at Les-Saintes-Maries-de-la-Mer. It has also been said that the boat included amongst its passengers Mary the mother of James the Less; Mary Salome, the mother of James and John; and Saint Sidonius.

The body of Mary Magdalen was said to be at Vézelay. Although this is some distance from Provence, it was said her body had been translated here in 745. However, a body discovered at the monastery of Saint-Maximin was declared to be hers. Her hermitage was said to be on the nearby mountain of St-Baume.

She is supposed to have had a child or children by Jesus, according to the Bloodline advocates, and the dynasty of Jesus was thus said to be the real Holy Grail. That the Cathars believed she had had an intimate relationship with Jesus was stated by Peter de Vaux de Cerney (13th Century) while Louis Martin in *Les Évangiles de Dieu* (1886) claims she and Jesus went to France and had a son. A manuscript dating from perhaps the 17th Century by William Spenser called *The Genealogy of Jesus Christ* was discovered in the National Library of Wales, which says Mary Magdalen became Jesus' assistant.

The story of her sojourn in France is dismissed by modern historians. The idea that Lazarus came there may be due to confusion with Lazarus, a 5th Century bishop of Aix, who spent some time in the Holy Land and died in Marseilles. As Mary Magdalen was identified by many with Mary the sister of the biblical Lazarus, this may have stimulated the tale of her migration.

**MARY OF BETHANY** In the Gospel of John, the sister of Martha and Lazarus. In the West she tended to be identified with Mary Magdalen*, a viewpoint that still has supporters. In the East she was usually regarded as a separate character and tradition says she died in Cyprus. Bloodline* advocates have regarded the two characters as one.

**MARY OF CLOPAS** A biblical character. She was present at the Crucifixion. A. Gilbert suggests the Virgin Mary had a son called Joseph who was identical with Clopas, to whom this Mary was married or of whom she was the daughter. Gilbert also argues for his identity with Barabbas. At the Crucifixion, he speculates, she got the blood of Jesus* on her and thus became the Grail*. The historian Hegessipus says that Joseph the carpenter had a brother named Clopas. This could be the same character, as Clopas was not a common name.

**MAZADAN** A character in Wolfram who was an ancestor of both Arthur* and Perceval*. He was married to a fairy called Terdelaschoye who came from Feimurgan. Actually, this betrays Wolfram's limitations when it came to French. *Feimurgan* is in origin the fairy's name, Morgan La Fée, while *Terdelaschoye* is Terre de la Joie, the country she came from.

However, Mazadan's name has oriental echoes which make us wonder about some of Wolfram's sources. Mazda was the benevolent creator of the Zoroastrian religion. Although he was the creator, he was not omnipotent. His name was generally prefixed with the title *ahura*. The Zoroastrian religion was the one which had obtained in Iran before the coming of Islam and it still has its votaries to this day, many of them in India. Zoroaster, who founded it, may have lived as long ago as BC 1800.

(Zoroastrians themselves incline to give him a date of BC 500). In later times, during the Sassanid era in Iran, an even higher god, Zurvan, said to be Mazda's father, was introduced to the pantheon. The question is where Wolfram might have obtained information about Zoroastrianism. There were, of course, some Zoroastrians left in Iran, but by then the majority of the inhabitants of that country were Muslims.There is a minor character actually called Zoroaster in Wolfram's poem.

**MELCHIZEDEK** Character in the Book of Genesis; a contemporary of Abraham. He was the King of Salem. The website Petragrail.tripod.com argues that the Hebrews had a special cup and it might have been the one used by Melchizedek. This went on to become the Grail*. Hebrew legend suggested Melchizedek was identical with Shem, the son of Noah.

**MELEAGANT** This knight was called *Melwas* in Welsh tradition, where he abducted Guinevere. He pops up occasionally in Grail* romance.

**MELES** A knight who went on the Grail* Quest. His name in Latin means 'badger'.

**MELIADUS THE WHITE** Not to be confused with others of this name in Arthurian tales, this was the name of a knight who went on the Grail* Quest.

**MELIAN** A knight who went on the Grail* Quest.

**MELKIN** A mysterious prophet whom John of Glastonbury quotes relating to Joseph of Arimathea*. He is supposed to have antedated Merlin.

The Latin in which this work is couched is not very susceptible to translation. The translation below is my own, made while referring to Armitage Robinson's.

John Leland (died 1552), Henry VIII's antiquarian, informs us that Melkin was once famous.

The prophecy runs:-

> The island of Avalon, avid for the death of pagans more than the rest of the world, by chanting spheres of prophecy decorated and for the future adorned, will be there praising the Highest. Abbadare, powerful in Saphat, of all pagans most noble, with countless thousands, has fallen asleep there.

> Amongst them Joseph, named of Arimathea, in a marble receptacle, has found perpetual sleep and lies on a bifurcated line [or in a shirt with two tails] next to the south angle of an oratory, made of wattles, for the worship of a mighty Virgin. Thirteen inhabitants of that place are there, their resting places indicated by the spheres mentioned above. For Joseph has within his sarcophagus two white and silver cruets, filled with the blood and sweat of the prophet Jesus.

> When this sarcophagus is found undamaged, it shall, in the future, be seen and shall be open to the entire world. After that, neither water, nor the dew of Heaven, will fail the inhabitants of that most noble island.

Meeting of Abraham and Melchizedek — by Dieric Bouts the Elder, 1464–67

> For a long time before the Day of Judgement in Jehosaphat, these things
> will be open and declared to the living.

This is very obscure material and I cannot vouch for the accuracy of its translation due to the peculiarity of its Latin. It has been suggested that there is a Muslim influence, due to the reference to Jesus as a prophet and to the fact that *Abbadare* has an oriental sound to it. This would probably mean it was an apocryphal work, dating from the time of the crusades. However, I do not find this convincing.

Leland tells us Melkin had undergone training as a bard. Bale writes of his knowledge of astrology and geometry. He was said to be the author of a number of lost works - *Historiola de Rebus Britannicis, De Arturii Mensa Rotunda* and *De Rebus Brytannicis.* That Melkin is to be identified with King Maelgwyn* Gwynedd is a contention which, I feel, is not proven. He was highly thought of by Capgrave, Hardyng and Leland. The idea of the opening of the sarcophagus leading to dew and rain in Britain may have echoes of a fertility cult practised in the area.

Margaret Murray had the idea that the Arabic work *Ketabu'l-Mikoyan* (Book of Kings) was the original book of Melkin.

**MELROSE ABBEY** A Cistercian house founded in Scotland in 1136. The heart of Robert the Bruce is said to be buried there. In the Prentice Pillar it is rumoured that the Grail* is to be found or, if not, that it might contain some indication of its location. Cf. Apprentice Pillar.

**MELYOS** A knight who went on the Grail* Quest.

**MENZIES** This Scottish clan (pronounced *Mingus*) may be part of the Grail Lineage* according to Dunford. This is inferred from a monument set up by Sir Alexander Menzies of Menzies as a tribute to his female ancestors in the Church of St Cuthbert at Weem.

**MERLIN**  The wizard's part in the Grail* stories is limited.  He made the Round Table in the image of that of Joseph of Arimathea* and stated that no one but the chosen knight should sit on the Siege Perilous*. He foretold the Dolorous Stroke*.  Lovelich lays emphasis on Merlin's rôle as one who prophesied the Grail.  The wizard may be based on an historical prophet and madman called *Myrddin* who flourished after the traditional Arthurian period.

**MEROVINGIAN GNOSTIC CHURCH** A religious denomination which holds that the Grail* Quest is the purpose of life. They believe in a God and Goddess. They hold that people were once gods and goddesses and that they go through various incarnations to learn the wisdom of the Grail.

**MEROVINGIANS** An early dynasty which ruled France from roughly 450-752 AD. They claimed descent from an eponymous ancestor named Merovech (?448-458 AD). This worthy, however, may not have been an historical person, but rather an ancient god. According to legend, his mother bore him to a beast which resembled a Quinotaur. This is implied rather than stated. A Quinotaur (below, drawn by Sir Francis Dashwood, notorious founder of the Hel Fire Club) looks as though some writer may have mistranscribed Minotaur, but it may have signified a five-horned bull. I might add that the beast concerned was a sea-beast and was not an actual Quinotaur, but something that looked like one, whatever that means. The whole legend did not appear until the 7<sup>th</sup> Century, in a chronicle ascribed to Fredegar.

Pierre Plantard* (1920-2000), founder of the Priory of Sion*, claimed to be of Merovingian descent, due to a secret bloodline which could be traced back to the Merovingian king, St Dagobert II (died 697). The authors of *The Holy Blood and the Holy Grail* seemed prepared to accept this, but went further. They suggested that the Merovingians were descended from the union of Jesus Christ* and Mary Magdalene*. Their Bloodline* was the Holy Grail*. Plantard distanced himself from the concept of the Grail bloodline in 1986.

**MEWIN** A Welsh writer who was credited with writing about the Grail*. There is no certainty that he is to be identified with Melkin*, as has been proposed.

**MIRROR** Lady Flavia Anderson contends that the Grail* was ultimately concerned with making sacred fire from the sun. A concave bowl of glass or crystal was used for this, the Grail Lance* being the beam of light from the sun which is necessary for ignition. She speaks of various sacred fires which, should they become extinguished, can only be relit from the sun. She further suggests the concave mirror could be the cauldron* of the Celts.

**MISSORIUM**  A portable altar-stone.  T. Sterzenbach argued that the original Grail* was one presented by the Roman general Aetius (died 454) to Thorismund, King of the Visigoths (reigned 451-3).

**MOLDAVITE**  A tektite, green in colour, found in the Czech Republic, possibly of meteoric origin. [The meteor is suspected to have struck Nördlinger Ries (Germany) 15 million years ago].  It has been associated by some with Wolfram's green stone Holy Grail*.  Moldavites actually qualify as jewels.  As such, they are sometimes called pseudo-chrysolite.

**MONTRÉALP-DE-SOS**  D. Roché identified this ruined castle in the Pyrenees with the Grail Castle*. This was presumably because a painting, found on the castle walls, was one also to be found in a 13th Century manuscript of the *Queste.*

**MONT-SAINT-MICHEL** (Manche)  Monastery in Normandy which P. Lavenu maintained was the major focus of Grail* romances.

**MONTSÉGUR** *see* Muntsalvaesch.

**MONTSERRAT**  The Grail* is said to be hidden under the monastery of Santa Maria de Montserrat in Spain.  The Nazis believed this and Himmler visited the Abbey in 1940, hoping to find it.  One assumes he didn't.

**MORDDWYD TYLLION**  (Welsh=pierced thigh)  A term applied, it is thought, to Bran* in the Mabinogi *Branwen.*  This would connect him to the Fisher King*.  Elsewhere, Bran is described as being mortally wounded in the foot.

**MORDRAIN**  Originally called Evelake*, this was the name he took on baptism.  *See* Evelake.

**MORDRED**  A personage in Arthurian legend, first mentioned in the *Annales Cambriae*, where we are told he and Arthur* fell at the Battle of Camlann.  Later legend claims he was Arthur's nephew.  A final tradition, which seems to be entirely literary in origin, appears in the *Mort Artu.*  This is to the effect that Arthur unwittingly committed incest with his half-sister, Morgause, and Mordred was their son.

In retellings of this version Morgause has been confused with her sister, Morgan Le Fay*, of whom she was probably originally a doublet.  L. Gardner in his Bloodline* theory says that a "ritual marriage" between brother and sister at Beltane was permitted amongst the Celts.  Arthur (who was part of the Bloodline) and Morgan performed such an act and as a result Mordred was born.  Because of his position in the Bloodline he was designated the Christ of Britain and Archpriest of the Sacred Kindred.  Clearly, this is all nonsense. M. Andere suggests that Mordiford in Herefordshire might be named after Mordred.

Sir Mordred

**MORGAN LE FAY**  This character is generally presented as an evil witch in Arthurian romance, but her origins tell a different story.

Morgan is generally thought to be a humanised form of the goddess *Modron*, who was worshipped by the Britons. She in turn was in origin the goddess *Matrona*. That Morgan was in origin a goddess seems to have been known to medieval writers, Giraldus calling her *dea phantastica* while in the poem *Sir Gawain and the Green Knight* she is referred to as 'Morgan the goddess'.

In the *Vita Merlini* were are told that Arthur, after his final battle, was taken to her dwelling, the island of Avalon*, where she lived as one of nine sisters, in order to heal the wounded king. These sisters sound very like the Nine Maidens* mentioned by Pomponius Mela and may also in some way be related to the Nine Hags of Gloucester and the various groups of stones in Britain referred to as Nine Maidens. Whether there were communities of Nine Women on islands in pre-Christian Britain cannot be determined. It may be there was a belief in a group of nine goddesses. These Nine Women are sometimes credited with a cauldron* and, while the *Vita Merlini* does not mention one in Morgan's case, as she was a healer who quite likely boiled up potions, it is at least possible she was credited with a healing cauldron which could have been a prototype of the Grail*.

We find in Chrétien's *Erec* that Morgan is described as Arthur's sister, but this would seem to be a later development. So too, apparently, was the evil character she showed in later Arthurian romances.

**MORTAIN** In the Church of St Evroult in this part of Normandy is an Irish casket of the 7th Century. It has been suggested it inspired a description of the Grail*.

**MOSES** One of the companions of Joseph of Arimathea* on his wanderings. In Robert he sat on a chair at the table which was purposely left vacant for Judas. For his temerity, he was swallowed up. In the *Estoire* he sat in the chair of Jesus* and he was carried away by flaming hands.

**MUNSALVAESCHE** The castle of the Grail* in Wolfram. Its name is merely a translation of Wildenberg, the place from which Wolfram came. It was located in the Forest Savage. Josephin Péladan (1858-1918) identified the stronghold with Montségur*. However, this cannot be the case, as Montségur was rebuilt by the Cathars* after Wolfram's poem was written.

# N

**NABON** A knight who went on the Grail* Quest.

**NAHMAD, CLAIRE AND BAILEY, MARGARET** Authors of the book *The Secret of the Ages* (2009), which claims to reveal the origins of the Grail*. Their beliefs involve the influence of the Annunaki*, the gods of ancient Iraq, in human history.

**NANTEOS CUP** A cup believed to cure sickness, resident for a time in Nanteos Mansion, Rhydyfelin, Wales, and identified as the Grail* apparently by E. Amery in 1905.

The legend concerning it is that seven monks from Glastonbury*, fleeing the minions of Henry VIII, brought the cup to Strata Florida, another monastery in Cardiganshire. The last surviving monk gave it to a member of the Stedman family, to be its custodian until the Church should claim it back. It was preserved by the Stedmans who passed it on to the Powells, whose house, Nanteos, was built in 1738. Pilgrims came to see the cup. It is now in a damaged state and it was said that this was due to people biting off pieces of the wood. Apart from being the Grail, it has also been suggested it was part of the True Cross.

Experts generally feel the cup is a mazar bowl, made of wychelm in the 14th Century. The cup is almost 5" in diameter and only the lower portion is intact.

The cup is now in a bank vault in Aberystwyth.

**NARTAMONGAE** A vessel of magical power in the folklore of the Ossetes. The modern day Ossetes are related to the ancient Sarmatians and tales of this vessel may have been brought to Britain by Sarmatians imported as part of the Roman army. Such an importation certainly occurred. Its story may have contributed to the Grail* mythos. The Nartamongae would not cook the food of cowards and inspired its owners. Its owner was Batraz, whom all acknowledged to be their unfailing leader. He shows a number of traits in common with Arthur*, to whom some of his legends may have been transferred.

**NASCIEN** The name taken by Seraphe* when converted to Christianity. It was he, the *Estoire* informs us, who first gave the Grail* its name, because it was agreeable. He looked into the Grail, as a result becoming blind, but he was cured by an angel with a lance.

After he had been cured, an evil personage named Galafres managed to have him and his son Celidoine* imprisoned unjustly. Nascien, however, was carried off in a cloud. Galafres, no doubt chagrined by this,

had Celidoine flung from the battlements. A number of disembodied hands saved him. Lightning struck the tower, killing Galafres.

Nascien, meanwhile, was taken to the Turning Island, which revolves in time to the heavens. He saw Solomon's Ship* approaching and, when it docked, he boarded it, but because of doubts which assailed him, the ship opened and Nascien fell into the sea. He made it to an island, where he was picked up by Celidoine, who had also boarded Solomon's Ship. They landed in the country of a giant of unfriendly bent and Nascien used the sword from the ship against him. It broke, so Nascien had to use another sword to wound the giant. They were joined by Mordrain and then told to leave the ship. Nascien, who ought to have known better, hesitated and was struck by a flaming sword.

Next messengers turned up, looking for Nascien. They were accompanied by the daughter of King Label*. Celidoine had converted her father when separated from Nascien. They landed on an island where there was a castle owned by Mordrain's son. A man in a white robe walked over the water and healed Nascien. Nascien sent messengers from the island to collect his wife, whom they brought back. Celidoine, meanwhile, had set off in a boat on the instructions of the white-robed man.

Joseph of Arimathea joined the company also by walking on water. They arrived in Britain where they found Celidoine.

The name Nascien is also given to the son of Narpus, one of Galahad's* ancestors, and to a contemporary of Galahad himself. The latter saw the Grail carried by a White Stag*.

**NICODEMUS** In the Bible, he helped Joseph of Arimathea* to remove Christ from the Cross. The occultist René Guenon in *Le Roi du Monde* (1925) says he accompanied Joseph to Britain. A legend preserved at the monastery at Fécamp (Normandy) said that he scraped blood from Christ and gave it to his nephew, Isaac. The latter placed the blood and knife in two leaden tubes and hid them in a fig tree.

The trunk was placed in the Mediterranean, whence it

floated to Normandy. It had grown three saplings on the way, which a holy man removed. An angel moved the trunk in from the shore. Some hunters found the trunk, but a force from it held them back. A chapel was built over it. In due course it opened. It has been suggested that Robert de Boron* based his Grail* poem on this story.

**NINE MAIDENS** In *Preiddeu Annwfn\**, which may be the prototypical Grail* quest, Arthur* and his followers go to the Otherworld, Annwn*, to obtain a magic cauldron*. This is tended by Nine Maidens, whose breath lit it. It is called the Cauldron of the Head* of Annwn, the word for Head (*pen*) here being susceptible to the meaning of either an anatomical head or a chieftain. It is also described as having a border blue with pearl. This puts us in mind of the fact that Geoffrey of Monmouth said Morgan* lived in Avalon* and was the chief of nine sisters. There can be little doubt that Annwn and Avalon refer to the same Otherworld*. Beliefs like this seem to stretch back to the First Century AD when Pomponius Mela wrote in *De Situ Orbis* that on the island of Sena (modern Sein, off the Breton coast) dwelt nine priestesses possessed of preternatural powers. He would have known of this through hearsay, as the further shores of Gaul were little known in Rome so early. It may be then that the original Grail was a cauldron and the Grail Maidens its Otherworldly custodians.

We may find a further echo of this in *Peredur*, where Perceval* sees a Head* instead of a vessel and discovers it is that of his cousin, slain by the Nine Hags of Gloucester. These seem to have been a tough bunch of beldames, but their number and the occurrence of the Head in their story may well tie them in with the Grail* saga. One of them had trained Peredur as a warrior and Arthur's men had quite a fight with them before they were killed off.

The curious fact is that the name Nine Maidens is given to groups of standing stones, some of which are not nine in number. Thus the Nine Maidens at Boscawen Un (Cornwall) actually consists of nineteen stones while that of Belstone Tor (Devon) contains eleven.

**NUMISMATICS** Certain coins and medals issued by Breton tribes show a vessel that may be a proto-typical Grail*. The tribes that issued them were the Unelles and Baiocasses

**OAK OF AVALON** Daniel Defoe, writing in 1724, says he was informed that an oak so-called had been planted where Joseph of Arimathea* landed. It is said there was once a grove of oaks in Glastonbury*, but the only ones left are the two called Gog and Magog.

**OLYMPIODORUS** (5th Century) Poet and historian, born in Egypt. He is supposed to have said that the Grail* was taken to Britain in the 5th Century, but this appears to be an error.

**ORDER OF THE GRAIL**

1 A modern order dedicated to mystic chivalry, it has been known by this name since 1985.

2 According to David Hughes *British Chronicles* (2007) there was an actual Order of the Holy Grail* in Arthurian times. This was a Church order, but Arthur* took it over. The Keepers or heads of the order had to be descended from Joseph of Arimathea*.

**ORDER OF THE RED GRAIL** A modern Wiccan organisation founded in Nebraska in 1993.

**ORTENAX** A fish found in the River Euphrates. A magical bone from it was used in the making of the Sword of Strange Hangings*.

**OSSENET** One of the knights on the Grail* Quest.

**OSWAIN** A knight who went on the Grail* Quest.

**OTHERWORLD** The Celts seem to have believed in an otherworld in which preternatural beings lived. Sometimes it was depicted as being overseas, but there appear to have been other entrances. This Otherworld in an Arthurian context seems to be the area variously called Annwn* and Avalon*. The preternatural beings were worshipped as gods before the coming of Christianity. It has also been suggested that the Grail Castle* was in fact conceived of as being in the Otherworld, as it has a tendency to pop up unexpectedly.

Surprisingly for some, the idea of a parallel universe is not repugnant to science. We do not have the technology, however, to drill our way into one, nor, at our present rate of scientific progress, will we be able to for millions of years. However, it cannot be ruled out that portals might already exist. For example, a scientific investigation at a ranch in Utah where paranormal phenomena were reported, described a wormhole leading apparently into another universe which appeared temporarily, the other universe being discernable.

If any such wormholes in fact exist, the question arises whether the identification of Avalon, an otherworld, with Glastonbury* might indicate the existence of a portal there.

M. Kaku (City University of New York) has argued that, billions of years hence, when this universe ceases to be habitable, we may have the technology to take ourselves to another.

In Welsh literature, when there are what seem to be proto-Grail expeditions, instead of using the Otherworld as their goal, the writers sometimes substitute Ireland*. This may be because the Otherworld was regarded as the home of the pagan gods, from whom they wished to distance themselves.

# P

**PALAMEDES** A Saracen knight, usually featured in Arthurian legend as a rival of Tristan* for the love of Iseult. He was converted to Christianity by Galahad* in the *Queste* and was present at Corbenic* at the Grail* Quest's end.

**PANTENE DE SERPENTINE** M. Oxbrow identifies the Grail* with this early dish at present to be found in the Louvre. It is green, embellished with small golden fish (a Christian symbol) and bedight with gems.

**PARCEVALS SAGA** Norse version of part of Chrétien's *Perceval*.

**PARENT** One of Joseph of Arimathea's* followers in the *Estoire*.

**PARTINAL** A knight who had used the Broken Sword* to kill the Fisher King's* brother in the *Third Continuation*. Perceval slew him and brought his head back to the Fisher King, who was thus cured.

**PARZIFAL** *see* Wolfram.

**PEEL CASTLE** A castle on the Isle of Man. It has been suggested this was the Grail Castle*, but it in fact dates only from the 11th Century.

**PELEUR** The name of the Maimed King* in the Welsh version of the Grail* story.

**PELLAM** The name of the Maimed King* in the *Lancelot-Grail*. According to L. Gardner, he had a daughter called Eglise* who married Pellinore* and became the mother of Perceval*.

**PELLEHAN** A variant form of Pellam*.

**PELLES** The name of the Fisher King* in the *Lancelot-Grail*. In *Perlesvaus* he was the brother of the Fisher King and was King of the Short Folk. There may be some connection here with Bilis, a character in Chrétien's *Erec* who was King of the Antipodes and lord of the dwarfs. In the *Prose Lancelot* he was Perceval's father. The *Tavola Ritonda* calls his realm Organia.

Hardyng says he ruled Vendotia, the north of Wales (i.e. Gwynedd). He may be derived originally from Pwyll in the *Mabinogion*. Another possible identification is with Beli Mawr, the Ancient British sun god.

**PELLINORE**  A king, said to be the father of Perceval*.  Pelles*, Pellam* and Pellinore have suspiciously similar names and those who see a Celtic mythological origin in the Grail* saga would suspect they are all derived from the Cymric ancestor god Beli Mawr.  On the other hand, his name may simply be an elongation of Pelles.  The fact that he is variously described as King of Listenoise* and the Wasteland* would seem to bear this out.  His mythological origins are again hinted at in the romance *Palamedes*, where he has a sister called the Lady of the Island of Fairies.

In the *Livre d'Artus* there are two Pellinores.  One is the Fisher King*, the other the ruler of the Grail Castle*.

**PENZANCE**  A town in Cornwall.  From here, according to *Perlesvaus*, the Grail* Quest started.

**PERCEFOREST**  A romance set in Britain before Arthur's* time, telling of Alexander the Great's installation of Perceforest as King of England.  The romance proceeds with British history until the arrival of the Grail*.  When Alan* arrived with the Grail, Gallafer, grandson of the king of Scotland, accepted Christianity.  He went to the Isle of Life, where Perceforest and others had been living and were still hale and hearty.  They were baptized, left the island and died.

**PERCEVAL**  The name of the original Grail* hero in the earliest poem on the subject we have, by Chrétien de Troyes*.  Chrétien's source was probably ultimately Celtic and the name *Perceval*, whether invented by Chrétien or some other, was likely to have been an approximation to the Welsh *Peredur**.  In a later romance, Perceval is called *Perlesvaus**.  In the German romance by Wolfram von Eschenbach, he becomes *Parzival**.

In Chrétien's *Perceval*, the hero was brought up in the woods by his mother.  He knew nothing of the world outside until he met three knights, who told him of Arthur's* court, whither he determined to go.  His mother gave him words of motherly advice, as mothers were in the habit of doing, then as now.  One of them was that, if ever he encountered a woman, he should take no more from her than a kiss and a ring.  This was really a rather foolish thing to say as, when Perceval came upon a woman sleeping in a tent, he woke her, gave her twenty kisses (rather exceeding mother's advice) and took from her an emerald ring.  He also scoffed some food in the tent before setting off once more.

When he reached Arthur's court (directions provided by a friendly charcoal-burner), he saw a knight in

red armour emerging. Going inside he found that this personage had threatened to attack Arthur and seize his kingdom. He had also spilled a goblet of wine over Queen Guinevere*, who was understandably miffed. Perceval pursued and overcame the Red Knight*.

He now set off on adventure. He received some training from Gornemant*, who then knighted him. He then came to the castle of the Fisher King*, where that monarch entertained him. Lying on the couch nearby was an aged figure, an old man who was clearly not in the best of health. The King presented Perceval with a sword. Into the hall came a mysterious procession, led by a young man carrying a spear dripping blood, followed by a damsel carrying a grail* and the another carrying a tailleor*. Perceval did not ask any question about the procession.

When he awoke next morning, the castle of the Fisher King had vanished. Perceval, no doubt nonplussed by this, set off once more and came to a damsel who wept bitterly and clutched a dead knight in her arms. She told Perceval that the Fisher King had been wounded through the thighs, but, if Perceval had asked about the grail*, he might have recovered.

Perceval returned to Arthur's court. There an ancient crone appeared and told him he should have asked about the nature of the Grail. Perceval set off once more, hoping to put right his mistake. He wandered for five years, in his eagerness quite forgetting about God, until he encountered a band of pilgrims, who reminded him. He came upon a hermit who told him his mother had died of grief at his departure.

Unfortunately, Chrétien never finished his poem, which would have left us all remarkably curious, had not a bevy of continuators told us what happened next.

The *First Continuation* was once, but is no longer, ascribed to a man named Wauchier. It mainly deals with adventures of Gawain* and Caradoc*, but when Gawain visits the Grail Castle* he is asked to mend a Broken Sword*, which he cannot do. We learn that this was the weapon that had wounded the Fisher King.

The *Second Continuation,* which may have been written by one Gauchier de Donaning, fills us in on the story of Joseph of Arimathea*. It also tells us that Perceval defeated the Demon of the Black Hand. Perceval had been told that the only way to restore the Broken Sword was to kill the murderer of the Fisher King's brother, which in due course he did. He became Grail King for a time, after which he became a hermit. He died after seven years and it is thought the Grail was taken to Heaven. A further continuation by Gerbert of Montreuill gives a somewhat different account of the mending of the Broken Sword and supplies Perceval with a wife named Blancheflor*.

The story of the Grail, which at some stage graduated from a common to a proper noun, is retold in different versions by a number of other authors.

Wolfram von Eschenbach's *Parzival* gives our hero's parents' names as Gahmuret* and Herzeloyde* and provides him with a half-brother named Fierfiz*. The story of this romance largely echoes Chrétien, but in this the Grail is, not a vessel, but a stone.

In the *Didot-Perceval* we meet Perceval's sister and we learn he is descended from Bron*. In *Perlesvaus* the might of the Round Table has declined. This may equate to the land's becoming a wasteland* as stated in the other romances. Perceval is a virgin in this work. According to this romance, the King of Castel Mortal* had killed the Fisher King and captured the Grail Castle. Perceval laid siege to this and the King killed himself. Perceval became Grail King, then a hermit and at last he sailed off to a wondrous island, which he had already visited once in the course of his adventures. Thither he had promised to return when a ship, with a red cross on its sail, came for him.

An English romance, *Sir Perceval of Galles*, tells the story of Perceval without an appearance of the Grail at all, though it does feature a gold cup* which performs a somewhat similar function. In this, Perceval not only kills the Red Knight, but the Red Knight's mother as well. Perceval's mother does not die and he marries Lufamour. His mother is Achefleur, sister of Arthur, in this composition.

In the *Lancelot-Grail*, the main Grail knight is Galahad*, while Perceval, though he attains the Grail, has a less prominent role to play. After achieving the Grail, he, Galahad and Bors* took it to Sarras*, where they were imprisoned, but they needed nothing other than the Grail, ever a supplier of sustenance, to nourish them. Galahad later became king of Sarras and, when he died, a hand from the sky took the

Grail away. A year and two months later, Perceval himself died. He had been leading an eremitical existence while Galahad was king.

The Welsh character Peredur is almost certainly identical with Perceval. His romance may contain a more primitive version of the Grail story, which will be delineated in the article dealing with him. *For the origins of this character, see under* Peredur.

**PERCEVAL'S MOTHER** Determined that her son should not die doing knightly deeds, she brought him up deep in the forest. When he finally left home, she died of grief. Perceval* was told that he was guilty of her death and this impeded his quest. In *Perlesvaus*, Perceval's mother is called Yglais. She is called Herzeloyde* by Wolfram and Philosophine in the Continuations.

**PERCEVAL'S SISTER** She accompanied Galahad* and Perceval on the Grail* Quest. When they came to Solomon's Ship*, it was noted the swordbelt they found, which was rightfully Galahad's, was worn, so she made him a new one from her hair. They came to a castle tenanted by a leprous lady, who required the blood of a passer-by to heal her and Perceval's sister donated her blood, dying as a result. The sister is unnamed in the *Queste,* but is variously called Dindrane (by Wolfram) and Agrestizia in the Italian *Tavola Ritonda.* In that work the lady of the castle is called Asperta Ventura and the castle itself

Verdoane. The Welsh version of *Perlesvaus* calls the sister Danbran. Welsh legend also gave Perceval another sister named Gwen.

**PERCHEVAEL** A 13<sup>th</sup> Century Middle Dutch translation of Chrétien's *Perceval*.

**PEREDUR** The hero of the Welsh version of the Grail* legend, dating from the 13<sup>th</sup> Century. Chrétien probably found the name of the Grail hero in this form and turned it into Perceval. When the Welsh romance of *Peredur* was composed, it is generally thought there was some French influence on it, but that the story contains much that is more primitive than the French versions. For one thing, there is no Grail, but a head. However, it could be said the Grail* is there, represented by the dish (*dysgl*) on which the head is carried, which corresponds in meaning to the word *graal* in Chrétien.

Peredur was the son of Efrawg, the Welsh for the city of York. It probably indicates his father was thought the ruler of that city. His mother brought him up secretly in the desert.

He visited his uncle's castle, where he saw a procession involving two youths bearing a spear with blood coming from it in three streams. A great wailing began, but despite the ululations, he did not ask what it was all about. Then entered two maidens carrying a bloodied head on a plate. This plate, as stated above, may be taken as the Grail. J. Grigsby feels that Peredur should have besought the Head* for information, perhaps by affixing his mouth to its.

Later on, Peredur was chidden by a Dark Maiden for not asking the question.

He underwent training with one of the Nine Hags of Gloucester. Afterwards, he discovered that the Nine Hags had killed his cousin and it was his cousin's head which had been carried on the plate. With the aid of Arthur* he defeated the Nine Hags in battle. These Nine Hags appear to have been warrior women and may not have been the crones their name implies.

Other adventures befell Peredur in the romance. He lived for fourteen years with the Empress of Constantinople and he fell in love with Angharad Golden-Hand. He is also supposed to have been in love with a damsel called Nef.

As to whether Peredur had an historical prototype, there were two British rulers of the 6<sup>th</sup> Century, Peredur and Gwrgi, who were twin brothers. They took part in the Battle of Arthuret, in which Merlin is said to have gone mad. It is possible that this Peredur was the original of our hero. He died in 580. Gruffydd Hiraethog said Peredur lived in Castell Cefail in Llangoedonor (Ceredigion).

**PERILOUS BED** When Gawain* came to the Grail Castle*, because he did not show sufficient reverence to the Grail*, when he slept in this bed he was struck by a fiery lance. He had a night of further adventures, which will be found in the article devoted to him.

Bors* also had a night in the Perilous Bed, where he heard a great crashing noise and a terrible wind. The windows rattled and a fiery lance struck him in the shoulder, but, as in Gawain's case, it was withdrawn. He had to fight a huge knight, whom he defeated. He then went back to bed only to be bombarded with arrows. He had to fight off a lion with distinctly unpleasant intentions and to witness a scene involving dragons and a leopard, just as Gawain had.

Then in came a man pale and thin, with two snakes around his neck, then an old man dressed as a priest carrying a lance dripping with blood, then twelve maids a-weeping and, just before midnight, he saw a light in the main chamber. He could not gain ingress, a sword preventing him. A bishop was there, with

a Grail on an altar. Bors couldn't find his way back to the Perilous Bed, which was perhaps just as well, bearing in mind the sort of things that happened when you were in it. He spent the rest of the night on the hall floor. In the morning, in came Pelles*, cheerful that no harm had befallen his guest.

Bors had obviously passed a test that Gawain had failed. Heinrich adds no one who had been evil could survive the test on the Perilous Bed.

**PERILOUS BRIDGE**  This was supposed to lead to the Grail Castle*. It is sometimes identified with Pomparles Bridge in Somerset. Indeed, this is referred to as *Pontem Periculosum* in 1344. Its appearance has changed somewhat in modern times.

**PERILOUS CHAPEL**  In the *First Continuation* both Perceval* and Gawain* came separately to a chapel where an altar light was extinguished by a black hand. This hand belonged to Satan, whom Perceval fought there in the *Second Continuation.*

**PERILOUS FOREST**  A forest which, if its name is appropriate, cannot have attracted many tourists and sightseers. In the *Lancelot-Grail*, Galahad* found a spring here. The water was bubbling and boiling, altogether very hot, and in its midst was the head of King Lancelot, his great-grandfather. Galahad managed to cool the water with his hands, as he was chaste. However, this episode could be used to further the argument that in some way a disembodied head* was connected with the Grail* quest.

**PERLESVAUS**  A 13th Century French Grail* romance, otherwise known as the *High History of the Holy Grail.*  Because of the bloodthirsty elements in the romance, N.L. Goodrich dubs the author a psycopath, but she may not mean it in the technical sense as defined by Dr Hare (University of British Columbia). R.S. Loomis voiced the opinion that he might have been slightly schizophrenic. H. Harrison says the author was Henry of Blois, perhaps using an original source, now lost, by Gildas*.

A picture that perhaps shows Gildas saying Mass before Joseph of Arimathea* and Nicodemus* was discovered at Chartres Cathedral in 1972. This is used in support of the argument for Gildas being an ultimate source.

There are some peculiar features about the work. The Grail Question* is not asked and Perceval's mother and sister do not die.

**PERRONIK** The hero of a Breton folktale, which seems to be connected with the Grail* Quest, perhaps even based on it. Perronik, the hero, managed to obtain a lance and a cup stolen by a wizard from the castle of Kerglas. He gave them back to their owner, a king, and the country prospered. The placename Kerglas (town of glas) seems reminiscent of Glastonbury*.

**PETER** One of the companions of Joseph of Arimathea*. In Robert, Joseph himself did not come to Britain, but sent Peter and Bron* to the Vale of Avaron, which may mean Glastonbury*. In the *Estoire*, however, Peter was wounded by Simeon*. His wound worsened and he took to the sea in a boat. He came to the Orkney Islands, where he converted King Orcant's daughter, whom he eventually married. He became the ancestor of Gawain* and his brothers.

**PETER, ST** Chief Apostle (painted by Rubens, opposite). G.F. Jowett feels he may have taught in Britain and taken the Grail* there. He thinks this would have occurred before he went to Rome.

He may have used as his source a statement by Simeon Metaphrastes (10th Century) that St Peter preached in Britain. Baronius (1538-1607) says he preached amongst the Britons about AD 58, following Metaphrastes. Cressy's *Church History of Brittany* (1668) also avers St Peter visited Britain.

**PHILIP OF FLANDERS** Philip was Count of Flanders from 1168-91. Chrétien tells us he obtained his account of the Grail* from a book of Philip's. This book is likely to have existed in reality, rather than being a mere literary device. Philip himself was a persecutor of heretics, so it is unlikely that Chrétien's source for his Grail story had an heretical element.

**PHOENIX** The legendary bird said to visit Egypt from its homeland in Arabia, mentioned by Herodotus, which was in later tradition said to be consumed by fire and to arise from its ashes. It was said to be the size of an eagle, partially red and partially golden. Wolfram said it accomplished its renewal by the power of the Grail*.

**PIERRE-ROGER DE MIREPOIX** During the siege of Montségur*, he was on the Cathar side and donned a suit of white armour. He then stood upon the battlements and terrified the attackers, who cried out that he was the Grail* Knight.

**PILTON** Place in Somerset where, according to local folklore, Joseph of Arimathea* built his second church.

**PINCADOS** A knight who went on the Grail* Quest.

**PLANTARD, PIERRE** (1920-2000) This Frenchman asserted, in what has now been revealed as a hoax, that he was the last descendant of the Merovingians* and, as such, true claimant to the throne of France. He had a confederate named Philippe de Chérisey*. They promulgated a story that certain documents supporting this had been found by Berenger Saunière*, a priest at Rennes-le-Chateau*. They

deposited certain documents concerning this in the Bibliothèque Nationale in 1967. These documents, known as the *Dossiers Secrets**, were supposed to have shown that the Priory of Sion* had been formed to protect Plantard's secret.

When *The Holy Blood and the Holy Grail* appeared, the authors asserted that the Merovingians themselves were descended from a marriage between Jesus* and Mary Magdalene*. At first Plantard did not deny this, but later he distanced himself from it. He disappeared from public life in 1974 and remained disappeared until his death.

**POUSSIN, NICOLAS** (1594-1665) French painter. His painting *Les Bergers d'Arcadie* (painted 1637-8) is currently in the Louvre. It depicts shepherds around a tomb bearing the Latin inscription *Et in Arcadia ego*, which perhaps indicates that Death visits even the pleasant land of pastoral Arcadia. In the Bloodline* theory, it was proposed that Poussin was one of the conspirators and the tomb was one on the Arques Road, near Rennes-le-Chateau*. Saunière* was supposed to have purchased two copies of the Poussin picture, but these have never been found. In fact, the tomb was only built in 1903. It was destroyed in 1988.

A marble bas-relied of Poussin's painting in reverse is to be found at Shugborough Hall (Staffordshire). It was made about 1750. There is an inscription there consisting of the letters OUOSVAVV having underneath it the letters D and M. This is obviously in code, but even the National Codes Centre at Bletchley Park has been unable to decipher it. Nonetheless, it is most unlikely to have anything to do with the Grail*.

**POWER POINTS OF THE GRAIL**  According to Nahmad and Bailey, these were Glastonbury*, Ur, a place in Mexico and a place in the Arctic.

**PREIDDEU ANNWFN**  A very obscure Welsh poem which may be an early version of the Grail* quest. Although generally referred to by this title, its proper full title is *Golychaf Wledic Pendevic Gulat Ri*. It bears some similarity to an Irish poem *Dún Scáith*. The poem's date can only be guessed - it could be anywhere from the 6th to the 14th Century. It tells how Arthur and a company venture to the Otherworld*. Although several different names are used for the Otherworld, they are probably all synonymous. The object seems to be the plunder of a cauldron*. This cauldron, it is suggested, is a proto-Grail. Taliesin* accompanied the expedition and is possibly the narrator of the poem.

The names used for the Otherworld are:

- *Caer Sidi*: perhaps the second word here is analogous to Irish *sídh*, which can either mean a fairy mound or the fairies themselves, many of these being full-sized warriors;
- *Caer Vedvit*: perhaps, fort where there is drinking of mead and feasting;
- *Caer Rigor*: fort of hardness
- *Caer Golug*: fort of ?
- *Caer Vendwy*: fort of God
- *Caer Ochren*: fort of enclosure.

Only seven return from the expedition.

It has been suggested that the poem refers to an expedition, not to the Otherworld, but to the Arctic. According to this theory *Caer Rigor* should read *Caer Frigor* (Cold Fort).

There are resemblances here to other similar tales thought to have had a bearing on the Grail. In the story of *Branwen* in the *Mabinogion*, Bran (accompanied by Taliesin) crosses the sea to Ireland, a substitute for the Otherworld. There is a conflict there involving a cauldron and only seven return. In *Culhwch ac Olwen* Arthur makes an expedition to Ireland (again, possibly a substitute for the Otherworld) to capture the cauldron of a giant.

It is possible all these stories are based on a single prototype of a quest for a supernatural cauldron which later developed into a quest for the vessel called the Grail.

**PRIORY OF SION**  An organisation founded in the 1950s by Pierre Plantard* (1920-2000), who wished to prove he was a descendant of the Merovingians* and, as such, claimant to the throne of France.

The Priory's own documents claim it was founded by Godfrey de Bouillon (died 1100) and from the Priory sprang the Templars*.

There was, in fact, an Abbey of Our Lady of Zion founded by Godfrey in 1099, but it was for an order of monks which did not outlast the 14th Century. The Priory documents claimed the Priory had separated from the Templars in 1168. Plantard's Priory was founded on May 7th, 1956.

The Sion in question is not Zion in Israel, but Sion near Annemasse (Haute-Savoie).

**PRESTER JOHN** A legendary Christian priest-king, said to rule a vast domain in the East. His empire was ultimately identified with Ethiopia.

A letter purporting to come from Prester John arrived in Europe, perhaps about 1185, describing his kingdom in excessively mighty and fantastic terms, to the extent of claiming that he had 72 subject kings. G. Hancock suggested that the author was the Ethiopian emperor Harbay and the letter was written to discourage European intervention in his country, but Harbay's dates are difficult to determine. He was a member of the Zagwe dynasty and it cannot be said with certainty that he reigned at all. If he did, some lists say he ruled for a mere eight years. His brother Lalibela, who seems to have succeeded him, lived in Jerusalem for a time and was responsible for the magnificent cave churches which bear his name. Perhaps word of their magnificence may have contributed to the Prester John legend. In Wolfram Fierefiz* and Repanse* became the parents of Prester John. In the *Jungere Titurel*, the Grail* was ultimately taken to his realm.

**PRIORY OF THE GRAIL** Part of a modern interdenominational Christian Templar organisation, situated in Minnesota.

**PSEUDO-GRAIL** This is mentioned in *Jungerer Titurel*. It was located in Constantinople and was a duplicate of the Grail*, but in time people mistook it for the real thing. There seems to have been a real object behind this story, which was taken to Troyes in 1204. It was still there in 1610. It has now disappeared.

**PROTO-GRAIL CULT** H. Harrison has argued that the cult out of which the Grail* mythos grew was megalithic in origin. Light entered megalithic sites and fertilised them. The Grail itself was a fertility object.

**PUY DE DOME** A mountain in the Massif Centrale in France. Atop this, you will today find a television transmitter. There was a temple here in ancient times. It was dedicated to Mercury, but this may be a romanisation of some Gaulish god, such as Lugos. The temple was excavated in 1873. A.T. Vercoutre thought it might have been the Grail Castle*.

**PYRAMID OF ALBION** A configuration based on a number of manmade markers drawn on the map of Britain by M. Beckett. He feels that this is the Grail Castle* where the fourth dimension can interact with this one at certain times. He regards this fourth dimension as being the Otherworld*. He goes on to suggest that the Pyramid of Albion may have been laid out by visitors from the future. He argues that the Pyramid may be the object of the prophecy of Melkin*.

**PYRENEAN BOWL** J. Goering has argued that Pyranean bowls, which bore the image of the Virgin Mary and which started to appear about fifty years before Chrétien's epic, were probably the major inspiration for the Grail*. In fact, these bowls were called *grails* locally. They had tongues of fire emerging from them. Most of them are now in the Museo Nacional d'Art de Catalunya

**QUESTE DEL SAINT GRAAL** Part of the Lancelot-Grail cycle (13th Century) this deals with the actual search for the Grail* and introduces the character of Galahad*. It is thought to have been written under the influence of the Cistercians.

**QUESTING BEAST** A creature that seems to be allegorical in origin. It had the head of a snake, the body of a leopard, the hindquarters of a lion and the feet of a hart. It made the sound of thirty couple hounds questing (i.e., barking) in its belly. Merlin* said it was one of the adventures of the Grail*. It was pursued by King Pellinore*.

ARTHUR·AND·THE·QUESTING·BEAST

# R

**RAFACE** Knight who took part in the Grail* quest.

**RAHN, OTTO** (1904-1939) A German, he was entranced by mythological matter, such as the story of the Grail*. At university he studied the Cathars* and hoped one day to prove there was reality behind thew stories of the Grail in the form of an article in their possession.

In 1929 he went to France to search for the Grail. He spent time at Montségur*, which he identified as Montsalvaesch*. He then leased an hotel in Ussat-les-Bains and searched caves in the area, discovering strange meteorites, allegedly once used in religious services. He believed the Cathars and Templars* had been connected with later Freemasons.

He quitted Ussat in 1932. In due course he returned to Germany. He may have travelled to Spain and certainly did so to Italy.

Rahn's first book *Kreuzzeg gegen den Graal* (1933) was on the SS reading list for promotion and he became a member of that organisation in 1936. In that capacity he continued his search for the Grail.

He also went on an Arctic voyage, whose purpose has yet to be discovered. It may have been to search for archaeological remains of a German homeland. It may also have been connected with the theory that the earth was hollow, the interior accessible by the Poles.

Things changed when he was placed on duty at Dachau, which left him depressed, disillusioned and possibly disgusted. He submitted his resignation to the SS. He then went for a walk in the Tyrol in very snowy weather and died from exposure.

One rumour has it that he actually found the Grail and brought it to Wewelswburg*.

**RAVENGLASS** A village in Cumbria (pictured below in a photo taken by Ron Jones, and used courtesy of him and Wikimedia Commons), at the estuaries of the Rivers Esk, Mite and Irt. It may date from as early as the 1st Century AD. The Romans called in *Glannoventa*. It has been suggested that the Grail castle* was here.

Perhaps the *Raven*-element in its name connects it with Bran*, who may be the prototype of Bron*, the Fisher King*. The word *bran* meant a raven in Old Welsh.

**RED ARMOUR** This was the colour of the armour worn by Perceval*. In Wolfram, he obtained it by defeating Ither. It later seems to have been worn by Galahad*. It may have had some special significance, now unknown, for the prime Grail* achiever to wear.

**RED CASTLE** A fortified house in Angus, Scotland. It has been suggested it was the Grail Castle*, but only dates from the 12th Century.

**RED CROSS SHIELD** This should have rightfully been given to Galahad*, but was appropriated by King Bagdemagus*, whom Galahad had to overcome to obtain it.

**RED GIANT** The killer of Perceval's* uncle in *Perlesvaus*. He met his own death at the hands of Perceval's father, Alan*.

**RED KNIGHT**  The knight who insulted Guinevere and was later defeated by Perceval*. He came from a place called Quinqueroi.  There seems to have been some theme of a red opponent in the earlier Grail* saga, which survived in such incidents as Gron, King of the Wasteland, being killed by the Lord of the Red Tower in the *Third Continuation* and Alibran of the Waste City being killed by the Red Giant in *Perlesvaus*.  In a non-Grail story, Sir Gareth is said to have overcome, but not slain, the Red Knight of the Red Lands.

Jung and von Franz suggest the Red Knight may be a dark side or element of Perceval and his slaying may represent the repression of Perceval's darker emotions.  This is just how children lose a certain individuality by conforming to the social pattern.  The drive of these emotions are now subject to Perceval's ego.  We must ask ourselves, however, if ascribing a psychological element to this story in such a manner is really reading more into it than is there to be read.

**RELICS**  F. Laughton-Smith thinks the Grail* consisted of a number of relics, including the Cup of the Last Supper, which were sent to Britain for safekeeping and hidden.

**RENNES-LE-CHATEAU** (Aude)  A village in the south of France, population about 90, near the Spanish border.  The parish priest, Berenger Saunière* (1852-1917) became involved in building projects which led people to question the provenance of the money which had funded these.  This eventually led to the thesis of the book *The Holy Blood and the Holy Grail* that he had discovered that Jesus* and Mary Magdalene* had married and were the ancestors of the Grail bloodline*.  This was not in fact the case.

In M. Lamy's *Jules Verne: Initiate et Initiateur* (1984), the author claims the church in Rennes-le-Chateau has a secret door. It leads underground, where immortal superheroes dwell.

**REPANSE DE SCHOYE** In Wolfram, she was the Grail Bearer, sister of the Grail King Anfortas*. She eventually married Fierefiz* and they became the parents of Prester John*.

**REX DEUS** [Latin=King God] A supposed organisation of families descended from the Davidic royal line, from the Hasmoneans and from certain high priests in Jerusalem.

Author T. Wallace-Murphy claimed to have been approached by a man named Michael who belonged to this group. He also claimed there had been a girls' boarding school in the Jerusalem temple around the birth of Jesus* and that Jesus himself was the son of a priest named Gabriel. This is the origin of the Bloodline*. It will not withstand historical investigation.

The purpose of the Rex Deus is supposed teaching is to bring about Heaven on Earth and this is to be found in the Grail* romances.

**RIGAUT DE BERBEZIH** A Provençal troubadour, he perhaps flourished in the 12th Century and made allusion to Perceval*, the Grail Lance* and the Grail* in his work. It has been suggested he even wrote a Grail epic, which has not survived.

**ROBERT DE BORON** (12th Century-13th Century) Writer of the Grail* romance *Joseph d'Arimathie*. He may have written a further romance about Perceval*. He also wrote one about Merlin*. He hailed from Montbéliard. His is the first work to identify the Grail with the cup of the Last Supper.

**RODERICK** King of the Visigoths (reigned 709-711). He was killed fighting the Muslims.

T. Sterzenbach thinks he was the original Fisher King*.

**ROSSLYN CHAPEL** More correctly, this Scottish chapel is called the Collegiate Chapel of St Matthew. It was built by the Sinclair family, on whom the barony of Roslin (so spelled) was conferred in 1028. The family were ultimately of French origin. The building was started in 1456, but only the choir and the Lady Chapel were completed. There is a crypt underneath and one of the objects said to lie in it is the Grail*, another the head of Christ.

A well-known myth is that the Templars* were connected with the Sinclairs* and brought the Cathar* secret to Scotland, sailing from La Rochelle after the fall of Montségur*.

Such a fleet never made its way to Scotland, the head of the Sinclairs at the time was married, so he could not have been a Templar, and the Sinclairs in fact testified against the Templars. Nonetheless this has not stopped people asserting that scrolls dug up by the Templars in Jerusalem found their way to the castle and that the Sinclairs were guardians of the Rex Deus* kings of Scotland.

Another suggestion is that the remains of Mary Magdalene* repose there, while various theorists have argued for the presence of the Ark of the Covenant*, the genuine Stone of Destiny (as opposed to the one resting in Edinburgh Castle, which is branded a fake), an extraterrestrial spacecraft and even a portal

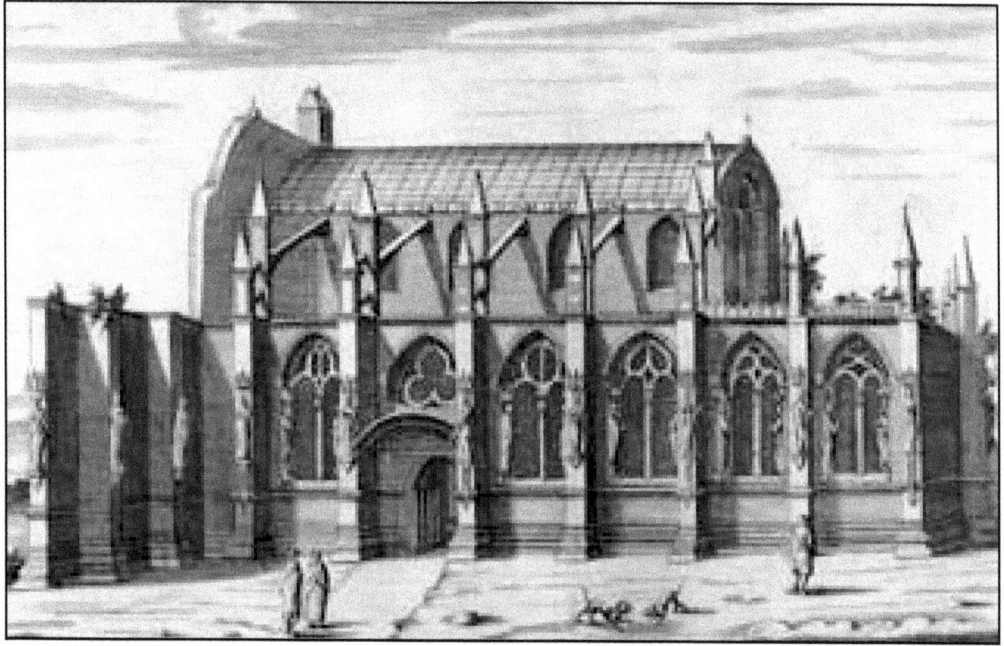

leading to another dimension. We can, I feel, dismiss the legend that Asterius the Pict founded the first settlement at Roslin, as Asterius sounds a most un-Pictish name.

In sum, if Rosslyn Chapel is connected with the Holy Grail, it cannot be linked with it through the Templars.

**ROUND TABLE** Arthur's* Round Table first appears in the *Roman de Brut* of Robert Wace (1155), its purpose to prevent quarrels over precedence. The Anglo-Saxon writer Layamon in his *Brut* says there was a fight over precedence and a carpenter from Cornwall fashioned the table to ensure there would be no repetition.

Grail* lore says it was made as one of three successive tables - the first, the Table of the Last Supper, the second the Grail Table* while the Round Table itself was the third. It was made by Merlin* for Uther, Arthur's father, and seated fifty knights. The *Didot-Perceval*, on the other hand, claims there were thirteen seats at it. One of the seats was the Siege Perilous*, whereat only the best knight in the world might sit.

The Round Table may not have been conceived as it is usually depicted. It may have been hollow in the centre, with the knights sitting on the inside. There is some doubt that the king himself would have been thought of as sitting at the table.

TVENDO TVVM POPVLVM

THE HOLY

MARTYR
NECTAN

ORA PRO NOBIS DOMINVM

ET NVNC ET IN PERPETVVM

NECTANE CONSORS MARTIRVM

# S

**SACRO CATINO**  A bowl made of green glass, formerly thought to be emerald,  in Genoa Cathedral. Some have said it is the Grail*. Jacob of Voraigne did so in his *Chronicon Januense.* It was captured by Crusaders in the East in 1101.

**ST JOSEPH'S WELL**  A well in Glastonbury Abbey*, one supposes called after Joseph of Arimathea*. When one Matthew Chancellor (18th Century) drank from it, he claimed to have been cured of asthma. A spa set up afterwards had water piped from Chalice Well*.

**ST NECTAN'S KIEVE**  A stream in Cornwall.  According to local lore, the Grail* Quest started from here.  Arthur* stood on a rock bridge above the stream while his knights below vowed to undertake their quest.  St Nectan's Kieve is situated in St Nectan's Glen.  St Nectan himself  (opposite) is said to have had his hermitage above the waterfall in the 6th Century.

**ST PATRICK'S ISLE**  An island off the coast of the Isle of Man.  N.L. Goodrich feels Joseph of Arimathea* took the Grail* to Peel* on the island.  T. Whiston argues that the Grail may have been kept on an altar on the island.

**SALVATERRE**  In the *Jungerer Titurel* of Albrecht, we learn that this was the country in which the Grail* was kept until it was moved to greater safety in the land of Prester John*.

**SAMITE**  A rich material used by royalty in the Middle Ages.  It is found in association with the Grail*; for example, there is a cloth of red samite on the Grail table in the *Queste.*

**SAN LORENZO FUORI LE MURA**  A basilica in Rome, dating from the 6th Century.  A. Barbagello, an archaeologist, claims the Grail* may be buried here.  In 1938 G. Da Bra, a Capuchin friar, identified the Grail with a terracotta funnel in a room in the basilica.  Mosaics and frescos in the building depict the cup of the Last Supper.

**SARACENS**  In Arthurian romance, this term seems to be used for pagans and the unbaptised generally, so when they are mentioned, it should not be assumed they are turbaned individuals.  In one romance they are described as worshippers of the sun, moon and planets.

**SARAH**  A personage regarded by Romany Gypsies as a saint.  It is said she came with Mary Magdalen* to France, but she is not mentioned in written works before the 15th Century.  Margaret Starbird has argued she was a child of Jesus* and Mary Magdalen, thus part of the Grail* Bloodline*.

There is a somewhat different Romany legend about her.  In this, she was a chieftainess of a Gypsy tribe who dwelt by the Rhône. When she saw Mary Magdalen and her companions coming, she realised their boat might overturn. She threw her cloak on the water and floated out on it to aid them. She helped them get to shore. However, it must be borne in mind that there were no Romany in France at the time of Mary Magdalen.

The connection between Sarah and Mary Magdalen seems to be pure legend. Sarah is called in Romany *Sara e Kali*, 'Sara the Black' and it has been suggested she is a christianised form of the Indian goddess Kali, the Romany being ultimately of Indian origin.

**SARRACINTE**  Christian wife of Evelake*.

**SARRAS**  A city which Arthurian romance locates between Babylon and Salvandre. In fact, the word seems to be a back-formation from *Saracen*, so its name can be taken as meaning "non-Christian city". It was the city ruled by King Evelake*. It contained a Temple of the Sun. It was once ruled by a giant named Alchendic, according to the *Prophecies de Merlin*. A previous ruler, whom Evelake had displaced, was called Holofernes. Evelake was succeeded on the throne by Aganor. Its richest city was Oriant. N.L. Goodrich has suggested it might have been Marseilles. L. Gardner opts for Gaza. M. Murray identifies it with Sers al-Liyaneh in Egypt. It might, opines Flavia Anderson, have been Glastonbury*. M. Gaster feels it may come ultimately from *Xerxes*, the name of a number of Persian kings. A. Gilbert suggests Salamis. August Hunt feels that Sarzeau in Brittany may be intended.

**SAUNIÈRE, BERENGER** (1852-1917)  This cleric became parish priest of Rennes-le-Chateau* in 1885. He restored the old church and it was re-consecrated by the bishop in 1897. Building work was carried out by the Giscard company. In 1901 he erected a series of buildings - the Villa Bethanie, Tour Magdala, a belvedere and gardens. From time to time Saunière appeared to have considerable sums of money and this was to lead to speculation that he had found some secret. An article in *La Depeche de Midi* (January 12th, 1956) suggests it was the treasure of Blanche of Castile. A book entitled *L'Or de Rennes* (1967) by Gerard de Sède* claimed one of the pillars in the church had been hollow and had contained two parchments.

Later the supposed parchments were produced. It was subsequently discovered they were forged by Philip de Chérissy*.

The book *The Holy Blood and the Holy Grail* maintained that Saunière had discovered a secret - that Jesus Christ had married Mary Magdalene* and their descendants had been the Merovingians*. This afforded him the opportunity to extort money from the Vatican*.

In fact, the source of Saunière's wealth was trafficking in Masses. He resigned in 1909.

**SCARPONNOIS**  An old French county, now in the département of Meurthe-et-Moselle.  It has been suggested the Grail Castle* was here.  In fact, the district was inhabited from early times.  There was a Gallo-Roman settlement called *Scarpone* at this place.  This would make it eligible.

**SCRYING**  The observation of objects by psychic means in glass, crystal, etc.  If you gaze at a crystal ball for long enough, it is possible to see some form of vision which seems to be the result of an induced altered state of consciousness.  A priest gazing into a chalice and being absorbed in meditation might see visions giving the impression of illumination or revelation.  G. Ashe says that in this may lie the origin of the Grail* experience.

**SECOND CONTINUATION** *see Chrétien de Troyes.*

**SECRETS OF THE GRAIL**  In Robert, secrets taught by Christ to Joseph of Arimathea*.  He taught these to Bron* in due course.  When some sit at the Grail Table* and experience what it provides, they are unable to express their experience to others.

The Grail romances seem to be full of deliberate obfuscation, merely for the sake of heightening the sense of mystery.

**SERPENT GRAIL**  Gardner and Osborn have suggested that the original Grail* was a receptacle, perhaps a human skull, in prehistoric times.  This was filled with a mixture of snake venom and blood, aiding t-cell replication.  This makes the immune system more effective.  The two authors would identify the Grail with the Elixir of Life and the Philosopher's Stone.

**SETH**  A biblical character, son of Adam and Eve.  The occultist René Guenon says the Grail* was originally given to Adam, but it was too holy to take from the Garden of Eden.  Seth was allowed to go back to the Garden to retrieve it.  It has been suggested by E.C. Brown that Galahad* replaces Seth rather than Perceval in the Grail Quest.  The Bible does not name Seth's wife, but the apocryphal Book of Jubilees says it was Azura.  V.P. Jones makes the unlikely suggestion that Seth founded the druids.

**SEVEN BRANCHES OF THE HOLY GRAIL**  These were recounted in the *Elucidation* by Perceval* to the Fisher King*.  They were as follows:-

- 7th - the Lance of Longinus*
- 6th - events of the labour
- 5th - anger and loss of Huden
- 4th - story of Heaven
- 3rd - goshawk that affected Castrars
- 2nd - story of the loss of Lancelot's* virtue
- 1st - adventure of the shield

What some of these are supposed to mean is, I suspect, anybody's guess.

**SHROUD OF CHRIST**  There was a legend that Joseph of Arimathea* brought the Shroud in which Christ was buried to Britain and pieces of it were still in Glastonbury* in historic times, according to T. Escott, in a work published in 1908.

**SHROUD OF TURIN**  It has been suggested by D. Scavone (University of Southern Indiana) that this famous Shroud was the original Grail*.

Unfortunately, there are objections to such an hypothesis, notably regarding the age of the Shroud.

Writing in the *Catholic Encyclopedia* (1907-12), the Jesuit Herbert Thurston takes a somewhat negative view of the relic. He points out that witnesses in the 15th and early 16th Century commented on the brightness of the Shroud, while it was now darkened. How would it have stayed bright from the time of Christ to the 15th Century, yet dulled between 16th-20th Centuries? He mentions that in 1389 the Bishop of Troyes declared it had been made by an artist who had admitted painting it. He suggests it was never intended to be more than a painting, but popular belief turned it into a genuine relic of Christ.

Radio-carbon dating on a fragment of the Shroud carried out at Oxford University, Arizona University and the Swiss Federal Institute of Technology yielded a date between 1260-1390 with 95% confidence. There has been a response that the piece of cloth used might not have been part of the original Shroud, but a piece later added to it.

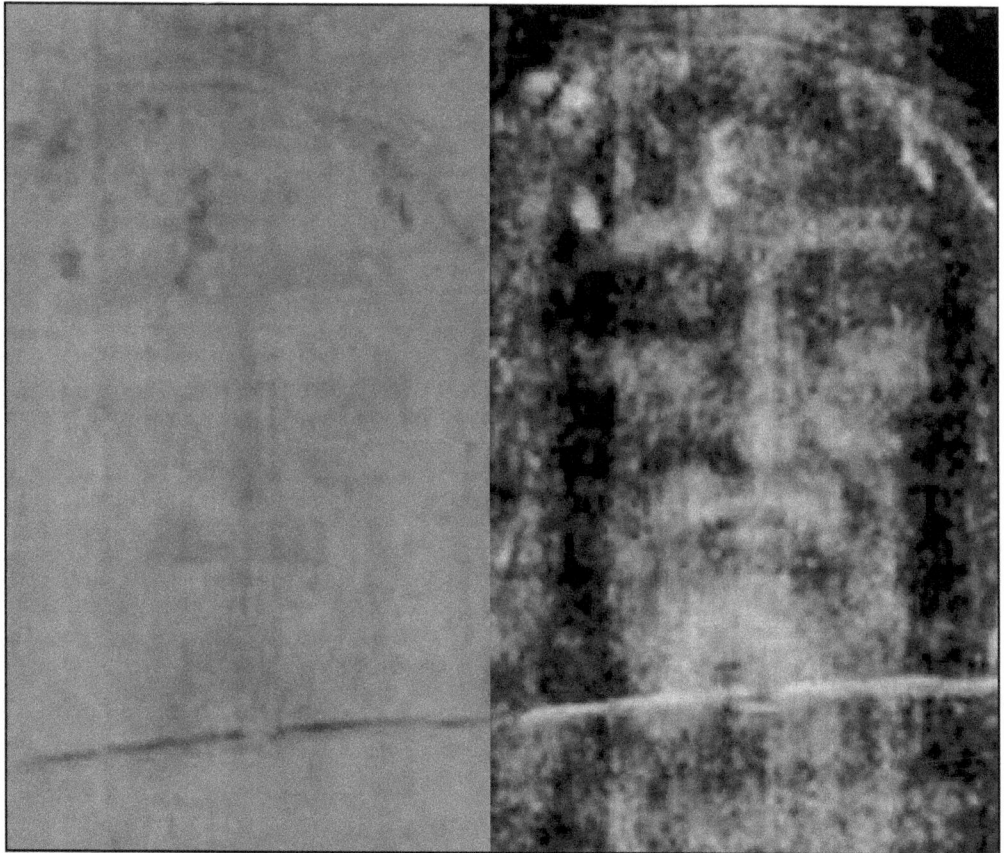

If the Shroud only came into existence after 1300, it can hardly have been the Grail. However, it must also be borne in mind that Raymond Rogers (Los Alamos) has dated the Shroud to 1400 to 3000 years ago.

A recent book by L. Buso claims the original Shroud was genuine, but, because it had become damaged, the present one is a copy made by Giotto di Bondone (1266-1367). He claims Giotto has left evidence on the Shroud to this effect. The theory that the Shroud was manufactured by Leonardo da Vinci* has also been put forward.

**SIEGE PERILOUS** This was the seat at the Round Table which Merlin* said was reserved for the best knight in the world. When Brumart, son of King Claudas, sat in it, he came to a sticky end. The gauche young Perceval*, arriving at Arthur's* court, jumped into it and split it. It had in fact been intended for him, but he shouldn't have assumed it. In later versions, the chair was for Galahad*, not Perceval. On the day he arrived, the doors and windows of Arthur's hall closed and a hermit led him inside, where he claimed the chair. Hardyng added the detail that Arthur was able to sit at it as well.

**SIEGE REDOUTEZ** In the *Queste*, a seat at the Grail Table*. It was intended for Josephes* and none other.

**SIGISBERT** The son of St Dagobert II*, King of Austrasia. According to standard history, he was murdered at the same time as his father in 679. The *Holy Blood and the Holy Grail* argued that he escaped and fled to Razès, becoming the father of the Grail* bloodline.

**SIGUNE** When Perceval* left the Grail* castle for the first time, he encountered her, cradling the form of her dead paramour. She upbraided him for not asking the Grail Question*. Wolfram* tells us that her name was Sigune, which had not been revealed before. He further informs us that Perceval at length buried her beside her lover, Schionatulander. Sigune is the name given today to a minor planet in the solar system.

**SIMEON** One of the companions of Joseph of Arimathea*. The Grail* refused to serve him, so he wounded Peter* in anger and was buried alive in punishment.

**SIMON ZELOTES** One of the Twelve Apostles. (right) He is said to have been executed by the Romans at Caistor (Lincolnshire) and the Caistor website claims he was recruited by Joseph of Arimathea*. Some have felt he was identical with the apostle Nathanael. Various traditions place his activities elsewhere.

**SINCLAIR, HENRY** (1345-1400) The scion of a noble family in Scotland.

In Frederick Pohl's book *Prince Henry Sinclair* (1974), he is credited with having made a voyage to Nova Scotia in 1398, where he became the original of the Glooscap of the Micmacs. This idea was based on a manuscript called *Two Commentaries* (1558) by Niccolo Zeno.

It dealt with how his father and uncle took service with a prince named Zichmi, whom Pohl identifies with Sinclair, and voyaged into the Atlantic. The story is generally regarded as a fraud by historians.However, M. Bradley has contended that the voyage took place to find a refuge for the Bloodline* of the Grail*, after the dissolution of the Templars*. He further suggests that Sinclair buried some treasure in the famous Money Pit on Oak Island, which has defied numerous attempts at excavation, because of the ingenuity of its construction.

Linked to this, Bradley feels there are ruins on Nova Scotia which would repay investigation. There is an Oak Island on either side of the province, as though they were marking a site. Oaks are not usually found on islands, as acorns do not float, so Bradley feels they were deliberately planted to signify the existence of something perhaps relevant to the Grail to be found there.

Two objects are cited as an indication that Sinclair's voyage may have taken place. One is the Newport Tower at Newport (RI), but this is in fact quite likely a 17$^{th}$ Century construction. The other is the supposed carving of a knight at Westford (Mass.), but this is thought by archaeologists to be no more than marks caused by erosion.

**SMITH, JOSEPH, JR (1805-1844)**   The founder of the Church of Jesus Christ of Latter Day Saints, commonly referred to as the Mormons.  Smith claimed to have received divine revelation.

V.G. Swanson argues that Smith was, genealogically, a Grail King*. He holds the Grail* as a bloodline and that Smith descended from the twins Zerah and Perez mentioned in the Old Testament.

The genealogical table he produces is untrustworthy, but it leads to Jesus* who, it is claimed, married Mary Magdalen*. They had a son who was the ancestor of Joseph Smith Sr and a daughter who was the ancestor of his wife, Lucy Mack Smith. Their son was Joseph Junior.

In the 19$^{th}$ Century, there seems to have been a belief among some Mormons that Jesus was a polygamist, his wives including Mary of Bethany* and Martha. However, Mormons often tend to identify Mary Magdalen with Mary of Bethany.

**SOLOMON'S SHIP**   King Solomon of Israel (BC 961-922) was informed he would have a famous descendant, for whom he determined to leave some artefact worthy of him.  At his wife's suggestion, he made a special ship.

Wood for the ship came from a twig taken by Eve from the Tree of Life in the Garden of Eden.  The ship contained a bed.  On one side was a white beam, on one side a red.  A beam, in the centre of which was a green post, connected them.  This ship was later to be used in the quest for the Grail*.

F. Anderson suggests the ship was in fact a metaphor for a sacred vessel, containing the setting for the crystal which she identifies with the Grail*.

**SONE** *see* Galosches

**SOVEREIGNTY** R.S. Loomis feels the two maidens in the Grail Procession* represent Sovereignty and Vengeance, while D.D.R. Owen argues there is definitely a sovereignty myth in the legend.

Whomsoever the Grail serves becomes thereby the sovereign of the land. The Fisher King/Maimed King* is decrepit, his sovereignty is weakened and the land is waste, so he is in sore need of a top up. J. Markale contends that the women in *Peredur* stand for sovereignty.

Irish parallels of the sovereignty myth, which may have come from a proto-Celtic myth or even have been imported into Britain by the Irish dynasty in Dyfed or the settlement of the Irish in Gwynedd: a group of Laigin who left their name on the Lleyn Peninsula, have been cited in support of this. By way of Brittany such concepts may have reached France.

The first of these concerns Niall of the Nine Hostages, (below) a king of Tara who reigned in the 5th Century. He and his brothers encountered a crone with foul teeth, hook nose, disease-wracked body and green nails. Black as coal was her colour and her knees and ankles weren't anything to write home about either. They entreated her for some water from her well. She said she would allow them to drink only in return for a kiss. This was a bit much for the brothers, who decided to remain thirsty. Only Niall kissed her and she turned into a beautiful woman who said she was the Sovereignty of Ireland and the kingship would fall to him. She is compared with the Grail Maiden and, in her ugly form, with the Loathly Damsel*.

Another example of this occurs in the tale *Baile in Scál* concerning Conn Céadchathach, the ancestor-god of the Connachta, who were to provide royal lines of various Irish kingdoms. Conn was brought to a plain with a golden tree. He was ushered into a house where a golden-crowned girl sat on a crystal chair. Next to her she had a golden vessel and in front of her a silver vat with golden corners and a golden cup. The girl was the Sovereignty of Ireland. Near her, the god Lugh was seated on his throne. When the maiden asked to whom she should serve the ale in the cup, she was told to Conn. His dynasty was to rule Ireland.

**STEIN, WALTER JOHANNES** (1891-1957)  Austrian writer who tried to identify persons in the Grail* saga with known historical persons.

**SUMER**  A territory with inhabitants of undetermined race in the south of Iraq.  Their origin is somewhat mysterious, but they are generally thought of as the originators of civilization.  The Uruk Culture (commencing BC 4100) is regarded as Sumerian, but Sumerian culture may have developed from the Ubaid culture which preceded this.  If not, there is some mystery about where the Sumerians ultimately hailed from.  They called themselves "black-headed ones".  Their language is related to no known language on earth.

L.A. Waddell in *The British Edda* (1930) maintained that, by reading the Norse *Poetic Edda* he had determined that the original Grail* quest had taken place in Sumer.  It was led by Arthur, who was identical with Thor and Adam, and it was to destroy a serpent-worshipping cult that used a cauldron*.

He calls the prototypical Arthur *Dur*, a king whose name I have failed to discover in any historical work dealing with Sumer.  There was a common noun in Sumerian, *dur,* which meant a link or an umbilical chord, but I hardly think there is a connection here.

It must be said that Waddell's theory is very unlikely to be true.

It has been suggested that the Glastonbury Zodiac* was constructed by Sumerians, but there is really no evidence to support this.

**SWORD IN THE STONE**  This is not the famous sword drawn by Arthur*.  In the *Queste* a stone that looked as though it were made of red marble came floating along a river by Arthur's court.  There was a message on the stone saying it could only be drawn by the best knight in the world.  Galahad* drew it, thus supplanting his father in that title.  The sword had originally belonged to Balin*.  There may lie behind all this a tradition from mythology of the old king of the land handing over his sword to his successor.

**SWORD OF STRANGE HANGINGS**  A sword found by Galahad*, Perceval* and Bors*, not to mention Perceval's sister* on board Solomon's ship*.  It had once been the property of Solomon's father, King David.  Because the hangings had rotted, Perceval's sister replaced them with her hair.

In the *First Continuation*, the sword fell into the hands of Gawain* when he rescued a maiden.

# T

**TABULA SALOMONIS**  This artefact was captured by the Muslims when they invaded Spain in 711. T. Sterzenbach identified it with the original Grail*, which he said was the missorium* presented to King Thorismund, the Visigothic ruler of that country.

**TAILLEOR**  Carried in the Grail Procession*, this was a carving dish. Wolfram makes the mistake of translating this as *messer,* 'knife'. F. Anderson suggests it was a bowl-shaped silver mirror.

**TALIESIN**  Taliesin is usually regarded as an historical bard who flourished in the 6th Century. However, so many bizarre elements are found in poems attributed to him and he is the subject of such strange stories that certain scholars distinguish between an historical Taliesin and a mythical Taliesin. That such a distinction existed in the Middle Ages is difficult to sustain. It should be added that some of the poems attributed to him are deemed apocryphal.

A dialogue between Taliesin and Merlin* is found in Geoffrey's* *Vita Merlini.* This takes place after Arthur's* departure for Avalon*. There is also a dialogue between them in Welsh literature.

The story of how Taliesin obtained his gifts is told in *Hanes Taliesin*, written in but antedating the 16th Century. There may once have been several versions in existence.

Ceridwen* - whom some deem a British goddess - had a very ugly son called Afgaddu. This unfortunate was so ugly that, at the Battle of Camlann, no one would kill him, for they thought him a demon. To compensate for this, Ceridwen prepared a cauldron* for her son. The first three drops of liquid imbibed from this would confer inspiration. Drink any more and you would die.

She engaged one Gwion Bach to stoke the fire which heated this vessel. The three drops of liquid intended for Afgaddu fell on his finger and he sucked them, ingesting their gift. Ceridwen was hopping mad.

Gwion, to avoid her anger, changed himself into several creatures to escape her and she turned herself into several other creatures to destroy him. Eventually, he turned himself into a grain of wheat and she turned herself into a bird and swallowed him. Nine months later, she gave birth to him as a baby. After this unusual gynaecological occurrence, he was given the name of Taliesin.

He became chief bard to Elffin and confounded the bards of Maelgwyn. He claimed that he hailed from the land of the Cherubim and was amongst the gods before Dôn gave birth to her son Gwydion. He had

hobnobbed with such gods as Math and Gwydion. He had been both dead and alive. He had also been such useful tools as the pin of a pair of tongs and an axe.

In the poem *Kat Goddeu* (Modern Welsh *Cad Goddeu*) we hear how he killed a scaly beast with an hundred heads. His interaction with biblical and historical persons was also interesting - he was with God at the fall of Lucifer, he carried the banner for Alexander the Great, he was patriarch to Elijah and Enoch, was the foreman at the Tower of Babel and was with Jesus* in the manger and, he adds, there was no marvel he could not unravel.

Taliesin takes part in and is indeed the narrator of two of the proto-Grail* journeys. He was in the expedition of Bran* to Ireland and in that of Arthur* to the Otherworld* in *Preiddeu Annwfn*. In the Middle Ages both these expeditions - the same story apparently in origin - were separated by centuries. What sort of being the early Welsh considered Taliesin to be cannot be fathomed.

It is possible, even likely, that Taliesin was a god in origin. However, there may also have been a 6th Century bard who bore his name. Perhaps the place called *Bedd Taliesin* (Ceredigion) is the site of his grave.

It has been suggested by Professor T.D. Griffin (Southern Illinois University at Edwardsville, St Louis) that *taliesin* (radiant brow) was actually a title, awarded to different poets at different times.

The very nature of the Taliesin material causes puzzlement. Thus E. Davies *Mythology and Rites of the British Druids* (1809) felt he had learned Hebraic lore.

As a purely personal suggestion, one wonders if Taliesin was the original Grail quester and that he accessed the contents of the cauldron at the culmination rather than the outset of his career. This would assume, however, that the cauldron* of Ceridwen was one of plenty as well as one of inspiration.

**TAMAR** According to L. Gardner and Nahmad and Bailey, a daughter of Jesus* and Mary Magdalen*. She was, according to Nahmad and Bailey, the full measure of the Grail*. Gardner says she was also called *Damaris* and married St Paul.

**TARA BROOCH** A brooch found in 1850 in Meath, Ireland, and generally dated to about 700 AD. According to the theories of R. Cotterell, it was at once stage in the hands of King Arthur* and its esoteric aspect enabled him to identify the Ardagh Chalice* as the Grail*.

**TAROT** A deck of cards which seems to date from the 15th Century. They were originally playing cards and were not used for occult purposes before the 18th Century. The word is derived from Italian *tarocchi*. They came to be used for fortune telling purposes by Romany Gypsies and others. A pack usually numbered 78 cards. At first, only the court cards were painted, but subsequently all were. J.B. Vaillant *Les Roms* (1857) thought the Romany actually invented the pack, but this seems to be incorrect.

A.E. Waite felt the Grail* and Tarot cards were linked. The Grail suits of cup, lance, sword and dish equated to the Tarot cups, wands, swords and pentacles. (He may have mistaken *pentagrams* for *pentacles*).

Waite designed a special Grail Tarot painted by Pamela Coleman Smith.

Amongst those who argue for a link between the Grail and the Tarot, there are those who say the Fool is Perceval*, the Hanged Man is the Fisher King*, the Tower is the Wasteland* and the moon is the Grail bearer.

If there is a link between the two, it seems tenuous to say the least, as the Grail appeared on the scene a long time before the Tarot. The origin of any linkage cannot be pinpointed.

**TAVOLA RITONDA** An Italian work (14th Century) which recounts Arthurian adventures, including Grail* adventures, from various sources.

**TEMPLARS** The Poor Fellow-Soldiers of Christ and the Temple of Solomon was a military order of monks, intended to protect pilgrims venturing to the Holy Land. In modern times it has been asserted that the Templars were involved in a Grail* cult, but this is not substantiated by any medieval documents. The rule of the order dates from 1129 and a papal bull *Milites templi* (1144) supports them. However, G.E. Lessing (1729-81) felt there was a connection between the Templars and the Grail Knights of romance. F. von Schlegel (1772-1829) echoed this in a lecture in 1812. J. von Hammer-Purgstall (1774-1856) felt the Templars had revered the Grail. The idea that the Templars were Gnostics seems to have been first postulated by F. Nicolai (1733-1811).

The Templars were arrested in 1307 by King Philip IV of France, charged with heresy. One of the charges brought against them was that they worshipped a head called Baphomet. This seems to have been a cover for the king to get his hands on their money. There was an investigation and Pope Clement V, though very much under Philip's influence, concluded they were certainly not heretics. However, Philip pressurised him into disbanding the order.

The Inquisition documents concerned involve no mention of the Grail. Despite this, modern conspiracy theorists feel there is good evidence that they were involved in some kind of Grail cult. The Templars were put on trial. At their trial one John of Châlons said some of them had escaped with eighteen galleys filled with treasure. A Scotsman called George Frederick Johnson (18th Century) opined that they might have gone to Scotland. The truth is that any who escaped from France are likely to have been small in number. The legend that a contingent of Templars fought at the Battle of Bannockburn between England and Scotland is not supported by contemporary documents.

The idea that a Templar fleet sailed from La Rochelle to Scotland, carrying the Grail* Bloodline* has been trumpeted by modern Grail conspiracy theorists, but tends to depend on very flimsy evidence. There is no record of a Templar fleet at La Rochelle. The Sinclairs of Roslin, who according to some, favoured the Templars, were certainly not amongst their supporters: indeed, two of them gave evidence against the Templars. It is said that the cross shaft at the grave of William Sinclair is a Templar one, but this is not the case. The Rosslyn* Chapel is also unconnected with the Grail.

One of the ideas that the Templars were connected with the Grail arises from the fact that Wolfram calls the Grail knights *Templeisen*. This term, however, means simply 'temple guardians' and would not have evoked images of the Templars in Wolfram's era. Indeed, one of the Hapsburgs founded an order called the *Templeist* somewhat later and no one even considered they constituted a re-formation of the Templars. The German word for Templars was not *Templeisen* but *Tempelherren*. On their shields they had a red cross, while Wolfram's *Templeisen* had a turtle dove.

On the whole, Templar connections with the Grail seem to be wholly the products of latter-day imagination. As already stated, there is no mention of a Grail in the Templar trials. That Freemasonry sprang from the Templars also seems a contention that rests on shaky foundations. The idea that the Templars were Gnostics seems to have first been postulated by F. Nicolai (1733-1811).

**TEMPLE OF THE HOLY GRAIL** A mystery school, perhaps founded in the 21st Century. It claims the Grail* antedates Christianity and that in the 9th Century it was placed in Europe under a Graalmeister to whom the title of Trevrizent* was given. The school claims to receiver its information from an Ascended Master called Hilarion, last seen in Tibet.

**TERRE FORAINE** A country containing or beyond the land of Listenois*.

**TERRE SALVAESCHE** The wild land where, Wolfram tells us, the Grail Castle* stood.

**THIRD CONTINUATION** *see* Chrétien de Troyes.

**THOLOMER** The King of Egypt and enemy of Evelake* in the *Estoire* (opposite). His name is doubtless based on that of the Ptolemy dynasty, who ruled Egypt before the Christian era. They had ceased to rule by the time in which the *Estoire* is set, Egypt in those days being part of the Roman Empire. The name of the king is a form of *Ptolemy*, the name of a dynasty which once ruled Egypt.

**THREE BROTHERS** Three knights, Alma, Luzes and Tanadal, who were all killed on the Grail* Quest.

**TIPPITT, SAMUEL** (born 1956) An Australian who claims descent from Mary Magdalen* and to carry the Bloodline* of Christ. He has the outline of a cross on his back and points out that this is a birthmark supposed in *The Holy Blood and the Holy Grail* to indicate Bloodline membership.

**TITUREL** We first find this name mentioned in *Erec*, a German romance by Hartmann von Aue. However, in German romance we learn he was the first Grail King*. His grandfather was Perillus, a convert to Christianity, who had a son named Titurison who married Elizabel and they begot Titurel. The Grail had been saved by Joseph of Arimathea* and an angel had brought it to Titurel. In Albrecht, the Grail was originally a stone, but a cup had been carved from it, used by Christ at the Last Supper. A dove placed a Sacred Host on it each Good Friday, which sustained the Grail company. It moved by itself and did not need a human hand to touch it. It placed itself in the sacristy of the Grail Temple* and had nothing but the air beneath it.

atant efuous · i · fergant qui fift for · i · grt
diestrier · et uint au roi · et dist madame
la roïne vous falue. Sire et si uos enuoie
nes lettres. Et li rois les prist · et uist

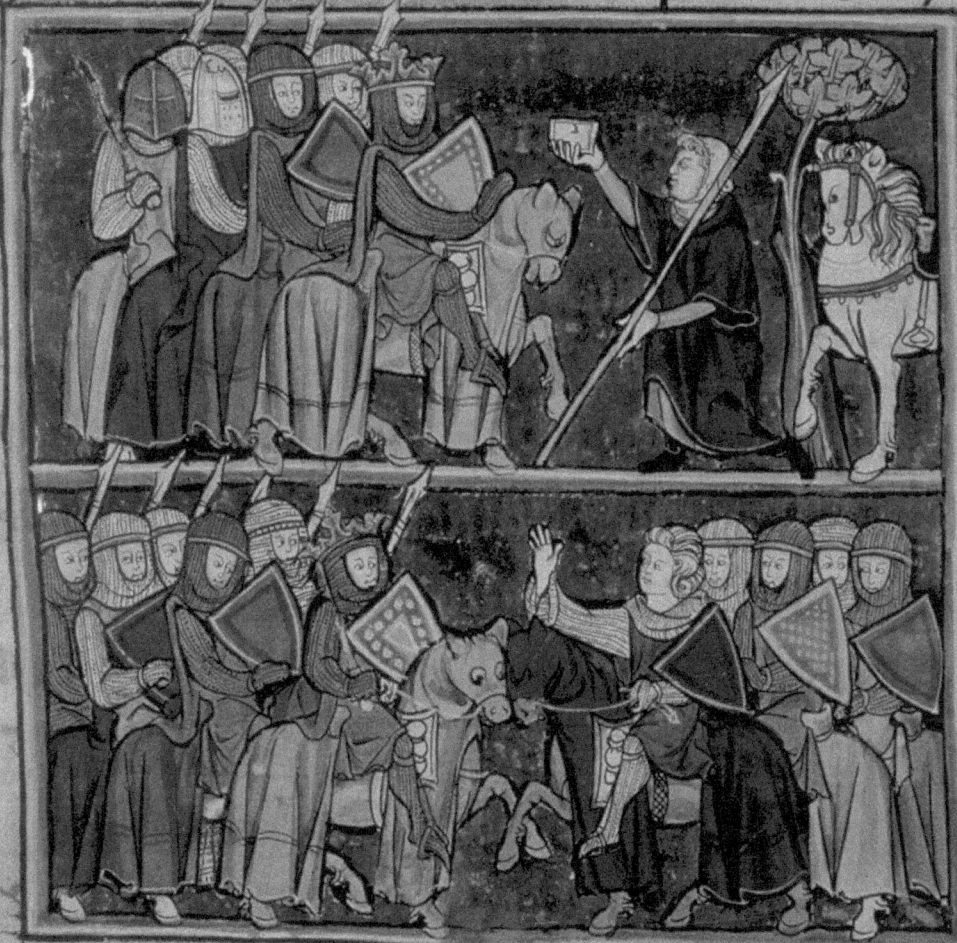

que fa feme le faluoit · Et que par la foi
que il deuoit queil feniflist del castel de
lincoine que tolomes le uoloit aseoir

After Perceval* had become Grail King*, he and Titurel decided to remove the Grail. Fearing the hostile countries surrounding Salvaterre*, they brought it to the land of Prester John*, where Titurel, at the age of 450, died.

**TOBLIER** Mentioned in the Grail Procession* in *Diu Crône,* this dish was fashioned of gold and jewels and contained three drops of blood.

**TRANSUBSTANTIATION** A Catholic term used in the Fourth Lateran Council in 1215, referring to the Real Presence of Christ in the Eucharist. R. Hutton argues that this provided the stimulus for the Grail* romances. In this, the present writer feels him to be mistaken, for, while references to the doctrine certainly appear in Grail romances, there is much in those romances that has no bearing on transubstantiation. However, the climate was probably right for the popularity of romances in which transubstantiation was a feature.

**TREBUCHET** The smith who had made the Broken Sword* and was the only one who could mend it, which he did.

**TREVRIZENT** Perceval's* tutor in Wolfram. He was a hermit and a brother of Anfortas*.

**TRISTAN/TRISTRAM** A famous Arthurian knight, known for his affair with Iseult. He occasionally features as a knight on the Grail* Quest. Although he is described as a Cornish knight, he is probably of Pictish origin.

According to the *Tavola Ritonda,* during the Quest he captured a castle named Ponteferno.

**TUATHA DÉ DANAAN** The gods of the ancient Irish. Once Christianity had been established, it was said they were a race that had inhabited Ireland in days of yore. They now lived in a parallel world. They seem to have been regarded as descendants of a vague background goddess called Dana, who was also known amongst continental Celts. She seems to be the equivalent of the Brythonic Dôn, wife of Beli Mawr. They came to be regarded as the fairies. They were said to have had four treasures, which may have gone into the Grail* mythos. These were the cauldron* of the Dagda (chief of the Irish gods); the spear of Lugh; the sword of Lugh; and the Lia Fáil or Stone of Destiny. The latter is still on the Hill of Tara in Meath. It is sometimes confused with the Scottish Stone of Scone.

**TURNING CASTLE** In *Perlesvaus* a castle seen by Gawain*, Lancelot* and Perceval*. The Turning Castle may be a motif akin to the Perilous Bed*. It was destined to keep turning until Christianity replaced paganism.

**TWELVE KNIGHTS** According to Hardyng, these discovered the Grail* with Galahad*, Perceval* and Bors*,

# U

**USSAT** (Ariège)  The final location of the Grail* according to Otto Rahn*.  The idea that the caves at Ussat were somehow connected with the Cathars* lacks historical evidence.  A. Gadal felt that to be a Cathar *Parfait* you had to go through initiations in these caves.  Gadal felt the Bethlehem cave at Ornolac was where these rituals were completed and that it contained the Grail* kept in a niche.  The current population of Ussat, a village in southwestern France, is 325.

# V

**VALENCIA CATHEDRAL** This cathedral in Spain (opposite) houses a red agate chalice with a golden stem set on an upturned bowl of red chalcedony. This is said to be the Grail*, sent from Rome to Spain by St Lawrence. Radio-carbon dating places it between the 4th Century BC and 100 AD. It is of Middle Eastern manufacture. It is on display at present.

**VALLE CRUCIS** A valley in Denbighshire which contains the ruins of Valle Crucis Abbey, founded in 1201 and dissolved by Henry VIII in 1537. The valley was called *Pantygroes* in Welsh. There is evidence that there were buildings earlier than the present abbey beneath it.

The possibility that it harboured an artefact identified with the Grail* has been suggested by the 15th Century Welsh poet Guto'r Glyn. In a poem dedicated to Robert Trevor (died 1453) who was buried at the abbey, he is referred to as being with the Holy Grail.
The Reverend H.T. Owen was given custodianship in the 19th Century. He found evidence of a Saxon building and also of Roman structures. Beneath this he found an oaken foundation. This could be part of a chapel founded by Joseph of Arimathea*.

**VESICA PISCIS** (Latin, 'bladder of a fish') A geometrical figure involving two intersecting circles, also known as a mandorla (Italian, 'almond'). It is sometimes thought to have an esoteric significance. From its shape it can be seen as a Grail*. There is one on the Chalice Well* cover in Glastonbury*. This was fashioned by Frederick Bligh Bond.

**VESPASIAN** Roman emperor 69-79 AD. According to Robert, he was healed of illness by the Veil of Veronica. As this was a Christian relic, he set off for Jerusalem to avenge the death of Christ and set free Joseph of Arimathea*, who was still imprisoned there. (The alleged Veil of Veronica is currently to be found in St Peter's Basilica, Rome).

In Albrecht's *Jungerer Titurel*, Vespasian was a progenitor of the Grail* kings as, through his daughter Argusilla, he was an ancestor of Titurel*.

**VULGATE VERSION** Name originally given to the *Lancelot-Grail*.

# W

**WALL** A village in the West Midlands. A. Gilbert contends this was the original Glastonbury*, being once called *Glastunum*.

**WASTE CHAPEL** Alternative name for the Perilous Chapel*.

**WASTELAND** The whole purpose of the Grail* Quest, at least initially, is the healing of the Wasteland. This is bound up with the condition of the Maimed King. In prehistoric cultures the fecundity of the land, on which agricultural communities depended, was bound up with the health of the king. Hence the wounding of the Fisher King/Maimed King* - through the thighs, in the foot, probably euphemisms for castration - is reflected in the barrenness of the land around about. The asking of the Grail Question* would enable the land to flourish once more, for it will heal the king.

In prehistoric times, it is thought the king was actually killed with the onset of senectitude and replaced by a younger model, who would be more fertile. It has further been suggested that in due course the king, finding such an arrangement disagreeable, would hide for a day and a surrogate would be killed in his stead. Thereafter the skulking monarch would be considered as having been born once more. Various bodies preserved in bogs, it has been suggested, that have undergone the Triple Death - a death which has involved three woundings - bear testimony to this, especially as, in accordance with mythic drama, they were killed in liminal areas, a bog being neither land or water. Part of the ceremony they went through may have involved the drinking of an hallucinogenic potion, as traces of ergot have been found in their stomachs.

The person who drank from the Grail* may represent the king's surrogate and before that he may have been the king himself. The king, having imbibed, would then be beheaded, so his head could serve as an oracle. Thus in the stories of Bran* and Peredur* decapitated heads feature.

Although the above procedure has not been reported in Britain as it is a leftover from prehistoric times, yet myths from Celtic Europe and further afield have been adduced in favour of the widespread existence of such a practice and, bearing in mind the elements of the Grail ceremony, are likely to lie at the root of the Grail myth.

One might ask why the Grail story is set in the reign of Arthur*? It has been pointed out that, at the time when he is supposed to have reigned, there were sundry meteorological disturbances recorded, which in many cases would have laid the land waste. When the myth of the Grail had to be placed in an historical setting, this was the one chosen. According to researchers at Cardiff University, a comet exploded in the upper atmosphere in the 6th Century, causing conditions similar to those in a nuclear winter. This led to very cold summers from 536-540 AD - just in the middle of the traditional Arthurian period and enough to inflict severe damage on agriculture, creating something of a wasteland. Strange weather was not confined to Britain. Dimming of the sun about this time was mentioned by Byzantine historians Procopius and John of Ephesus. Darkening of the moon was mentioned by Zacharias of Mytilene and Cassiodorus Senator. Even in far-off China, the history *Nan shi* tells us of a great explosion's being heard.

**WEWELSBURG** A castle in Westphalia. Himmler set it up as an SS site in 1934. It was hoped to place the Grail* there, if Otto Rahn* found it. A rock crystal there is in fact said to have been regarded as the Grail. In 1945 the Germans blew part of the castle up, including the SS cadre building. After the War, the castle was restored.

**WHITE STAG** Such animals often occur in mythic literature. One led Perceval* to the Grail Castle*. Another - or perhaps the same one - with the Grail* between its antlers was seen by one of the characters named Nascien*. In *Perlesvaus*, there is a cart pulled by three white stags. In the Church of St Onenne in Tréheurenteuc in Brittany, which contains stained glass windows relevant to the Grail, there is a painting of a white stag wearing a golden cross with four lions round about it, painted on the church wall. White stags are not mythical. They are red deer (*Cervus elephas*) with a condition called leucism which, unlike albinism, whitens the skin, but doesn't redden the eyes.

**WHITEHAVEN** A town in Cumbria. It has been suggested that the Grail Castle* was here, but there is no evidence of settlement before the 10th Century.

**WHITNEY** Place in Herefordshire. From here came the Whitney family, who claimed descent from Peredur*.

**WICK FARM** Joseph of Arimathea* landed at this place in the vicinity of Glastonbury*, according to Somerset folklore.

**WILLIAM OF MALMESBURY** A competent historian of the 12th Century. He was of mixed Norman and Anglo-Saxon descent. Writing of Glastonbury* he said the Old Church was the oldest in England. In one version of his work there is a long but easily detectable interpolation. *See* Glastonbury.

**WOLFRAM VON ESCHENBACH** (1170-1220; dates approximate) A German poet of whom little or nothing is known. He wrote the Grail* epic *Parzival*. This was largely based on Chrétien de Troyes, but contains a number of differences. The major one is that the Grail here is not a vessel, but a stone. Wolfram did not name Chrétien as his source. Instead, he claimed to have obtained his information from a certain Kyot*, who had himself found it in an Arabic manuscript written by an astronomer called Flegetanis*. This pedigree is widely doubted by commentators, though some opine that Kyot was the troubadour Guiot de Provins (died 13th Century). There are some peculiarities about the poem with a possible suggestion of the orient, but one must treat Wolfram's claims regarding sources with hesitation. He seems to have had access to Celtic sources also. Gwrgi was the name of a brother of Peredur*, thought to be the Welsh equivalent of Perceval, and a Gurzgri turns up in Wolfram. So too does Mabonagrain, who would appear to be the Welsh Mabon. Wolfram claimed to be illiterate, but this itself may be a literary device.

# Y

**Y SEINT GREAL** A Welsh version based on the *Queste* and *Perlesvaus*, dating from the 13th Century.

**YONET** One of Arthur's* servants who was present at Perceval's* fight with the Red Knight*. As Perceval had no clue how to put on the latter's armour, Yonet helped him. Yonet may have originally been a more important character in the Grail* story.

**YVAIN** This is the French form of Welsh *Owain*. He is historical and actually lived a little after the traditional Arthurian period. He was king of North Rheged and died about 595. He is thought to have succeeded his father Urien, but it has been suggested that Urien outlived him. He is supposedly buried at the Giant's Grave, Penrith (Cumbria).

In the context of the Grail*, he observed the Marvels of the Grail. He was also supposed to have been a descendant of Joseph of Arimathea*.

**YVAIN THE BASTARD** The natural son of Urien of North Rheged. He went on the Grail* Quest and took part in a joust where Gawain* killed him, not recognising him.

# Z

**ZAMBOR** According to L. Gardner, he was one of the Grail* Bloodline*.

**ZAZAMANC** The kingdom in Africa or Asia ruled by Belacane*.

**ZILJE** In Wolfram, the place where Gahmuret* met Trevizent*. It is today called Celje in Slovenia.

**ZINGARO, ROCCO** (born 1941) Head of an organisation called the Ordine del Tempio, he claims to have the true Grail*. He claims it came from a Coptic monastery.

# EPIL⊕GUE

I t is not usually the function of reference books to try to reach conclusions. If the reference book should deal with something of a mysterious origin, such as the Grail, it is general practice to enumerate various theories regarding it, but not to speculate about which may be correct.

However, the present writer, being a self-proclaimed eccentric, does not feel himself bound by such conventions. He has a theory concerning the origin of the Grail which he intends to share with the reader, as no one else (to his knowledge) has put it forward before.

Having said this, the writer would stress that this is a theory and no more. Someone else, perhaps even brighter than the writer, may come up with a more convincing hypothesis.

That those who wrote of the Grail were not entirely sure of what they were writing about is, I think, fairly obvious. They would have no notion why the Fisher King/Maimed King's health might have affected the country around about. Why did his health depend on a question? What was the true significance of the strange procession?

I feel the specifically Christian parts of the story are later accretions. Robert seems to be the one who identified the Grail with the Cup of the Last Supper. While he did not send Joseph to Britain, he opened the way for the author of the *Estoire* to do so. Masses witnessed are clearly influenced by speculation regarding transubstantiation, much discussed at the time; but what about the other parts to which no really Christian meaning can be assigned?

The Procession has characteristics which are definitely not Christian. The Grail is meant to be carrying the Sacred Host, but I feel safe in saying that, anterior to Christianisation, it carried something else. The Fisher King and Maimed King have both been wounded in the thighs and the general consensus is that this is an euphemism for castration. For two people living in the same castle to be castrated seems unlikely. Even in those far-off days, castration was hardly commonplace. I think we may see in these two persons a duplication of a single character, which may have occurred in the oral forms of the story.

But what is all this about fish anyway? The Fisher King may do a spot of angling to pass the time, but this is hardly enough to give him a name. If he played golf (which is, I suspect, perfectly easy to play if you have been castrated, but I cannot vouch for this from personal experience) they would hardly have called him the Golf King, any more than we call a bank manager who plays golf the Golf Bank Manager.

Moreover, Chrétien is eager to assure us that the Grail does not contain a fish, whether pike, salmon or lamprey. Could this mean that in the original version of the story a fish was indeed what it contained?

Let is now wend our way to Lydney Park in Gloucester, on the Severn Estuary. Here, a temple dedicated to the Celtic god Nodens was excavated by Sir Mortimer Wheeler in 1920. This contained some interesting motifs.

First of all, we shall look at the god Nodens, who was worshipped by the Ancient Britons. There have been various attempts to interpret his name. J.R.R. Tolkien of hobbit fame thought it meant 'to catch, to trap'. However the linguist J. Pokorny felt it meant 'catcher, fisher'. Here we have what may be a fisher-god, though I should warn the reader there have been various other interpretations of his name.

One of the representations in the Temple shows a triton and, facing him, a fisherman who has caught a salmon. Could it be that in the fisherman we have the prototype of the Fisher King and is he identical with Nodens?

It is here we must ask if there is any known tradition of Nodens' being castrated. There is none or, at least, none which has survived. However the whole point of the Fisher King's injury is that he has a blemish which renders the land waste. This was because he was lacking a physical part and, in Celtic belief, if a king had suffered any amputation or even blemish, the kingdom would lose its fecundity. The king was seen as married to his kingdom and had to be a perfect specimen for the kingdom to flourish.

Now Nodens was also worshipped in Ireland under the name of Nuada and, as such, was the king of the gods. Then he suffered a singular blemish: his arm was cut off and he had to surrender his crown. Eventually the god of medicine, Dian Cecht, made him an artificial arm out of silver and he was restored to power.

Nuada was associated with the River Boyne and this river was tenanted by the Salmon of Wisdom: whosoever ate it became, as one might guess, wise. Nuada was also called Elcmaire and we are told that the hero Cúchullain killed a salmon in the Boyne and then mutilated Elcmaire, thus making him unfit for king-ship.

If we try to put all this into some kind of coherent narrative, we might come up with something like this:-

*Nodens/Elcmaire was mutilated. The land was laid waste. The Sacred Salmon was brought in each night, but could not be served to him unless the Grail Question were asked. When he partook of it, served from the Grail, the health of Nodens was restored and with it the fecundity of the land.*

This was probably enacted as a ritual from time to time, as the procession has a ceremonial touch to it. It may have been enacted at the inauguration of a new king (the quester). There may have been some sort of initiation (the Perilous Bed). The temple at Lydney Park has indications that it was a healing centre, so the ritual was possibly witnessed by pilgrims. Other gods, such as Beli (?Pelles) and Bran (?Bron) may have been the foci of similar ceremonies.

What about the story of Joseph of Arimathea's voyage to Britain? All I can say is that it is not impossible that it occurred.

Could he have brought the Cup of the Last Supper with him? This is also not impossible, nor is it impossible that the two stories in due time coalesced.

The Grail remains a mystery.

# BIBLI⊕GRAPHY

## Primary Sources

- Bede *History of the English Church and People* Harmondsworth: Penguin, 1955.
- Chrétien de Troyes *Perceval* tr. N. Bryant. Cambridge: Boydell & Brewer, 1982.
- Coe, JB./Young, S. (ed.) *The Celtic Sources for the Arthurian Legend* Felinfach: Llanerch, 1995.
- *Complete Dead Sea Scrolls in English* tr. G. Vermes. Harmondsworth: Penguin, 2004.
- *Didot-Perceval* Seattle: University of Washington Press, 1966.
- Geoffrey of Monmouth *History of the Kings of Britain* translated by L. Thorpe. Harmondsworth: Penguin, 1966.
- Geoffrey of Monmouth *Vita Merlini* tr. J.J. Parry. Urbana: University of Illinois Press, 1925.
- Hardyng, J. *The Chronicle from the first beginning of England* Amsterdam: Theatrum Orbis Terrarum, 1976.
- Heinrich von dem Türlin *The Crown* tr. by J.W. Thomas. Lincoln (Nebraska): University of Nebraska Press, 1989.
- John of Glastonbury *Chronicle of Glastonbury Abbey* Woodbridge: Boydell & Brewer, 1984.
- *Lancelot-Grail* ed. N.J. Lacy. Cambridge: Brewer, 2010.
- Lovelich, H. *The History of the Holy Grail* London: Trübner, 1877-8.
- *Mabinogion* translated by J. Gantz. Harmondsworth: Penguin, 1966.
- Malory, T. *Le Morte d'Arthur* Harmondsworth: Penguin, 1969.
- Matthews, J, (ed.) *Sources of the Grail* Edinburgh: Floris, 1996.
- *The Nag Hammadi Library* ed. J.M. Robinson. San Francisco: Harper & Row, 1978.
- *Perceforest* translated N. Bryant. Cambridge: Brewer, 2011.
- *Perlesvaus* translated N. Bryant. Cambridge: Boydell & Brewer, 1978.
- Robert de Boron *Joseph of Arimathea* London: Rudolf Steiner Press, 1990.
- William of Malmesbury *The Early History of Glastonbury* tr. by J. Scott. Woodbridge: Boydell and Brewer, 1981.

# Secondary Sources

- Andere, M. *Arthurian Links with Herefordshire* Little Logaston: Logaston Press, 1998.
- Anderson, F. *The Ancient Secret* Wellingborough: Research into Lost Knowledge Organisation, 1987.
- Anson, P.F. *Bishops at Large* London: Faber, 1964.
- Ashdown, P. *The Lord was at Glastonbury* Glastonbury: Squeeze Press, 2010.
- Ashe, G. *Avalonian Quest* London: Methuen, 1982.
- Ashe, G. *Guidebook to Arthurian Britain* Wellingborough: Aquarian Press, 1983.
- Ashe, G. *King Arthur's Avalon* London: Collins, 1958.
- Baigent, M. (et al.) *The Holy Blood and the Holy Grail* London: Arrow, 1996.
- Barber, R. *The Holy Grail* Harmondsworth: Penguin, 2005.
- Bartrum, P. *A Welsh Classical Dictionary* Aberystwyth: National Library of Wales, 1993.
- Bathurst, W.H. *Roman Antiquities at Lydney Park, Gloucestershire* London: Longmans, Green, 1879.
- Benham, P. *The Avalonians* Glastonbury: Gothic Image, 1993.
- Benjamin, R. *The Seed of Avalon* Westhay: Zodiac House, 1986.
- Bernstein, H. *Ark of the Covenant, Holy Grail* Marina del Rey: DeVorss, 1998.
- Birks,W./Gilbert,R.A. *The Treasure of Montsegur* Wellingborough: Crucible, 1987.
- Bradley, M. *Holy Grail Across the Atlantic* Toronto: Hounslow Press, 1988.
- Bruce, C.W. *Arthurian Name Dictionary* New York: Garland, 1999.
- Bruce, J.D. *The Evolution of Arthurian Romance* Gloucester (Mass.): Smith, 1958.
- Caine, M. *The Glastonbury Zodiac* Kingston (Surrey): published by the author, 1978.
- Carey, J. *Ireland and the Grail* Aberystwyth: Celtic Studies Publications, 2007.
- Carley, J.P. *Glastonbury Abbey* Glastonbury: Gothic Image, 1996.
- Carley, J.P. (ed.) *Glastonbury Abbey and the Arthurian Tradition* Cambridge: Brewer, 2001.=
- Clébert, J.-P. *The Gypsies* Harmondsworth: Penguin, 1867.
- Codd, D. *Mysterious Somerset and Bristol* Derby: Derby Books Publishing Co., 2011.
- Coghlan, R. *Illustrated Encyclopaedia of Arthurian Legends* London: Vega, 2002.
- Cottrell, M. *The Celtic Chronicles* Timoleague: Celtic Press, 2006.
- Cressy, S. *Church History of Brittany* Rouen: privately published, 1668.
- Darrah, J. *The Real Camelot* London: Thames & Hudson, 1981.
- Dunford, B. *The Holy Land of Scotland* Glenlyon: Sacred Connections, 2002.
- Dunning, R. *Glastonbury* Stroud: Sutton, 1994.
- Fanthorpe, L. and P. *The Holy Grail Revealed* North Hollywood: Newcastle, 1982.
- Freedman, H. *The Gospels' Veiled Agenda* Winchester: O Books, 2009.
- Gardner, L. *Bloodline of the Holy Grail* London: Element, 1996.
- Gardner, L. *Genesis of the Grail Kings* London: Bantam, 1999.
- Gardner, P./Osborn, G. *The Serpent Grail* London: Watkins, 2005.
- Gibbs, R. *The Legendary XII Hides of Glastonbury* Felinfach: Llanerch, 1988.
- Gilbert, A. *The Holy Kingdom* London: Bantam, 1998.
- Godwin, M. *The Holy Grail* London: Bloomsbury, 1994.

- Gold, N. *The Queen and the Cauldron* n.p.: published by the author, n.d.
- Goodrich, N.L. *The Holy Grail* New York: HarperCollins, 1992.
- Greed, J. *Glastonbury Tales* Bristol: St Trillo, 1975.
- Green, T. *Concepts of Arthur* Stroud: Tempus, 2007.
- Griffen, T.D. *Names from the Dawn of British Legend* Felinfach: Llanerch, 1994.
- Grigsby, J. *The Wasteland* London: Watkins, 2003.
- Haag, M. and V. *The Rough Guide to 'The Da Vinci Code'* London: Rough Guides, 2004.
- Hake, L. *Something New on Men and Manners* Hailsham: printed by J. Breads, 1828.
- Hancock, G. *The Sign and the Seal* London: Heinemann, 1992.
- Harrison, H. *The Cauldron and the Grail* Volume 1. San Francisco: Archives Press, 1970.
- Hopkins, M. (et al.) *Rex Deus* Shaftesbury: Element, 2000.
- Hughes, D. *British Chronicle* Westminster (Md.); Heritage, 2007.
- Hunt, A. *The Secrets of Avalon* London: Avalonia, 2010.
- Hutton, R. *Pagan Religions of the British Isles* Oxford: Blackwell, 1991.
- Hutton, R. *Witches, Druids and King Arthur* London: Hambledon & London, 2003.
- Jackson, A. *In Search of Arthurian Kings* Bloomington: author house, 2006.
- Jones, V.P. *Glastonbury Myth or Southern Mystery?* Hayling Island: Rosamund House, 1999.
- Laughton-Smith, F. *Britain, Christ and the Dhamasutra* Vol. 1 Bristol: A.A.A. Publishing, n.d.
- Lacy, N.J. (ed.) *The New Arthurian Encyclopedia* London: St James Press, 1995.
- Laidler, K. *The Head of God* London: Orion, 1999.
- Lewis, H.A. *Christ in Cornwall* Falmouth: Lake, n.d.
- Lewis, L.S. *St Joseph of Arimathea at Glastonbury* Cambridge: Clarke, 1955.
- Loomis, R.S. *Celtic Myth and Arthurian Romance* London: Constable, 1994.
- Loomis, R.S. *The Grail: From Celtic Myth to Christian Symbol* London: Constable, 1992.
- Loomis, R.S. (ed.) *Arthurian Literature in the Middle Ages* Oxford: Clarendon Press, 1961.
- MacKillop, J. *Dictionary of Celtic Mythology* Oxford: Oxford University Press, 1998.
- Mann, N.R. *Isle of Avalon* St Paul: Llewellyn, 1996.
- Markale, J. *The Grail* Rochester (Vt.): Inner Traditions, 1999.
- Matthews, J. *Taliesin* London: Aquarian Press, 1991.
- Matthews, J./Green, M. *The Grail Seeker's Companion* Wellingborough: Aquarian Press, 1986.
- Michael, B. (et al.) *Dictionary of Ethiopian Biography* Volume 1 Addis Ababa: Institute of Ethiopian Studies, 1975.
- Michell, J. *New Light on the Ancient Mystery of Glastonbury* Glastonbury: Gothic Image, 1990.
- Moore, M. *The Masters of the Mystical Rose* Cairns (Queensland): Triad, 1999.
- Morgan, R.W. *St Paul in Britain* Oxford: Parker, 1861.
- Nahmad, C./Bailey, M. *Secret of the Ages* Chieveley: Capall Bann, 2009.
- Odelain, O./Ségineau, R. *Dictionary of Proper Names and Places in the Bible* London: Hale, 1982.
- Ó hÓgáin, D. *The Lore of Ireland* Cork: Collins Press, 2006.
- Olschki, L. *The Grail Castle and its Mysteries* Manchester: Manchester University Press, 1966.
- O'Rahilly, T.F. *Early Irish History and Mythology* Dublin: Dublin Institute of Advanced Studies, 1946.
- Oxbrow, M./Robertson, I. *Rosslyn and the Grail* Edinburgh: Mainstream, 2005.

- Palmer, K. *Folklore of Somerset* London: Batsford, 1976.
- Paton, L.A. *Studies in the Fairy Mythology of Arthurian Romance* Boston: Ginn, 1903.
- Peebles, R.J. *The Legend of Longinus in Ecclesiastical Tradition and its connection with the Grail* Boston: Furst, 1911.
- Petit, S.L.I. *Discovering, at last, King Arthur* n.p.: published by the author, n.d.
- Phillips, G. *Search for the Grail* London: Century, 1995.
- Pickford, D. *Magic, Myth and Memories in and around the Peak District* Wilmslow: Sigma, 1993.
- Picknett, L./Prince, C. *The Templar Legacy* London: Bantam, 1997.
- Pohl, F. *Prince Henry Sinclair* New York: Potter, 1974.
- Porter, H.M. *The Celtic Church in Somerset* Bath: Morgan, 1971.
- Putnam, B. *The Treasure of Rennes-le-Chateau* Stroud: Sutton, 2005.
- Rhys, J. *Studies on the Arthurian Legend* Oxford: Clarendon Press, 1891.
- Roberts, A. (ed.) *Glastonbury: Ancient Avalon, New Jerusalem* London: Rider, 1978.
- Sinclair, A. *Discovery of the Grail* London: Century, 1998.
- Sinclair, A. *Sword and the Grail* London: Century, 1993.
- Stone, A. *The Bleeding Lance* Loughborough: Heart of Albion Press, 1992.
- Stone, A. *A Splendid Pillar* Loughborough: Heart of Albion Press, 1992.
- Stout, A. *The Thorn and the Waters* Frome: Green and Pleasant Publishing, 2008.
- Street, C. *London's Camelot and the Secrets of the Grail* London: Earthstars, 2009.
- Swanson, V.G. *Dynasty of the Holy Grail* Springville: Cedar Fort, 2006.
- Taylor, J.W. *Drama of the Lost Disciples* London: Covenant, 1968.
- Treharne, R.F. *The Glastonbury Legends* London: Cresset, 1967.
- Tribbe, F. *The Holy Grail Mystery Solved* Lakeville: Galde Press, 2003.
- Vickery, A.S. *Holy Thorn of Glastonbury* St Peter Port (Guernsey): Toucan Press, 1987.
- Waddell, L.A. *The British Edda* n.p.: Chapman & Hall, 1930.
- Waite, A.E. *The Hidden Church of the Holy Grail* London: Rebman, 1909
- Waite, A.E. *The Holy Grail* London: Rider, 1933.
- Walters, J.C. *The Lost Land of King Arthur* London: Chapman & Hall, 1906.
- Welborn, A. *Decoding Mary Magdalene* Huntingdon (Indiana): Our Sunday Visitor, 2006.
- Weston, J.L. *From Ritual to Romance* New York: Smith, 1920.
- Whitehead, J. *Guardian of the Grail* London: Jarrolds, 1959.
- Williams, J. *Glastonbury Abbey; its history and ruins* Wells: Green, 1869.
- Wood, J. *Eternal Chalice* London: Tauris, 2008.
- Wright, R. *A History of Castle Eden Lore in Search of King Arthur* Hartlepool: published by the author, 1985.

# APPENDIX ⊕NE

## Bibliography of Grail Fiction

In this bibliography, fiction about the Grail features, but it does not claim to be complete. Most of the works listed are in prose, though there are a few poems and some drama. Dates given are those of publication of the edition cited or of copyright.

- Ashley, M. (ed.) *The Chronicles of the Holy Grail* London: Robinson, 1996.
- Attanasio, A.A. *Kingdom of the Grail* London: HarperCollins, 1994.
- Barjaval, R. *L'Enchanteur* Paris: Denoel, 1984.
- Bennett, N./Elrod, P.N. *Keeper of the King* Riverdale: Baen, 1997.
- Benoit, P. *Montsalvat* Paris: Michel, 1957.
- Bischoff, D. *Star Spring* New York: Berkeley, 1982.
- Bradley, M.Z. *Lady of Avalon* London: Joseph, 1997.
- Bradley, M.Z. *The Mists of Avalon* New York: Knopf, 1982.
- Brandstetter, A. *The Abbey* Riverside: Ariadne, 1988.
- Brewer, G.M. *The Holy Grail* Montreal: printed for the author at the Herald Press, 1933. [drama]
- Brown, D. *The Da Vinci Code* London: Bantam, 2003.
- Butts, M. *Armed With Madness* London: Penguin, 2001.
- Calvino, I. *Il cavaliere inesistante* Turin: Einaudi, 1959.
- Carr, J.C. *King Arthur* London: Macmillan, 1895.
- Carrington, L. *Le cornet acoustique* Paris: Flammarion, 1974.
- Chadwick, E. *Daughters of the Grail* New York: Ballantine, 1993.
- Chateaubriand, A. de *Le Réponse du Seigneur* Paris: Grasset, 1933.
- Chester, N. *Knights of the Grail* London: Nelson, 1907.
- Child, P. *Inspector Hadley - the Holy Grail Murders* Newport Pagnell: Benbow, 2011.
- Christian, C. *The Sword and the Flame* London: Macmillan, 1978.
- Clynes, M. *The Grail Murders* London: Headline, 1992.

- Cochrane, M./Murphy, W. *The Forever King* London: Millenium, 1992.
- Cohen, M. *Too Bad Galahad* Toronto: Coach House, 1972.
- Connor, K. *Cosmic Adultery* Leicester: Matador, 2011.
- Connor, K. *Fire Trial* Leicester: Matador, 2011
- Cook, S. *The Book of Galahad* Studio City: Empire Publishing Services, 2005.
- Cooper, J. *Ruth* London: Hutchinson, 1986.
- Cooper, S. *The Dark is Rising* New York: Atheneum, 1973.
- Cooper, S. *Greenwitch* London: Chatto and Windus, 1974.
- Cooper, S. *The Grey King* London: Chatto and Windus, 1975.
- Cooper, S. *Over Sea, Under Stone* London: Chatto and Windus, 1965.
- Cooper, S. *Silver on the Tree* London: Chatto and Windus, 1977.
- Cornwell, B. *Harlequin* London: HarperCollins, 2000.
- Cornwell, B. *Heretic* London: HarperCollins, 2003.
- Cornwell, B. *Vagabond* London: HarperCollins, 2002.
- Costain, T. *The Silver Chalice* London: Hodder and Stoughton, 1953.
- Coulter, C. *The Wild Baron* New York: Jove, 1997.
- Crompton, A.E. *Merlin's Harp* Naperville: Sourcebooks Fire, 2010.
- David, P. *Fall of Knight* New York: Ace, 2006.
- David, P. *One Night Only* New York: Ace, 2003.
- Dorst, T./Ehler, U. *Merlin oder das Waste Land* Frankfurt: Subkamp, 1981. [drama]
- Eliot, T.S. "The Waste Land" [poem] in *1905-1925* London: Faber and Faber, 1925.
- Fisher, C. *Corbenic* London: Red Fox, 2002.
- Fleischer, L. *The Fisher King* London: Penguin, 1991.
- Furth, R. *Sherrilyn Kenyon's Lords of Avalon* New York: Marvel, 2009.
- Gash, J. *The Grail Tree* London: Collins, 1975.
- Gerard, F. *Secret Sceptre* London: Rich and Cowan, 1937.
- Gracq, J. *Le Roi Pecheur* Paris: Corti, 1951.
- Gracq, J. *Au Château d'Argol* Paris: Corti, 1939.
- Hanratty, P. *The Book of Mordred* Lake Geneva (Wis.): New Infinities, 1988.
- Harrison, H. *King and Emperor* London: Legend, 1996.
- Heiduczek, W. *Die selfsame Abenteuer das Parzival* Berlin: Neues Leben, 1974.
- Hemingway, A. *The Greenstone Grail* London: Voyager, 2004.
- Hill, P.S. *The Last Grail Keeper* New York: Holiday House, 2001.
- Hockney, M. *The Armageddon Conspiracy* n.p.: lulu.com, 2008.
- Holdstock, R. *The Iron Grail* London: Gollancz, 2007.
- Horowitz, A. *The Unholy Grail* London: Walker, 1999.
- Hunter, J. *Perceval and the Presence of God* London: Faber and Faber, 1978.
- Irvine, A. *One King, One Soldier* New York: Del Rey/Ballantine, 2004.
- Jenner, M. *Conundrum's Book* n.p.: lulu.com, 2008.
- Jewett, E.M. *The Hidden Treasure of Glaston* New York: Viking, 1946.
- Jones, F.H. *The Life and Death of King Arthur* London: Macmillan, 1930.
- Jones, G. *Bold as Love* London: VGSF, 2001.

- Kane, G./Jakes, J. *Excalibur!* New York: Dell, 1960.
- Katz, W.W. *The Third Magic* Vancouver: Greenwood, 1988.
- Lampo, H. *De heks en de archaeolog* Amsterdam: Muellenhoff, 1967.
- Lampo, H. *Wijlen Sarah Silbermann* Amsterdam: Muellenhoff, 1980.
- Lawhead, S. *Grail* Oxford: Lion, 1998.
- Llewllyn, S. *Abbot Dagger's Academy and the Quest for the Holy Grail* London: Puffin, 2008.
- Lowe, S. *In the Court of King Arthur* Racine: Whitman, 1918.
- McKenzie, N. *Grail Prince* New York: Del Rey, 2003.
- Machen, A. *The Great Return* Westminster: Faith, 1915.
- Machen, A. *The Secret Glory* London: Secker, 1922.
- Markale, J. *La fille de Merlin* Paris: Pygmalion, 2000.
- Massie, A. *The Evening of the World* London: Weidenfeld and Nicholson, 2001.
- Massie, A. *Arthur the King* London: Weidenfeld and Nicholson, 2003.
- Michaels, P. *Grail* New York: Avon, 1982.
- Miles, R. *The Child of the Holy Grail* London: Simon and Schuster, 2000.
- Mitchison, N. *To the Chapel Perilous* London: Allen and Unwin, 1955.
- Mittermeyer, H. *The Veil* New York: Warner, 1996.
- Monaco, R. *Parsival* New York: Macmillan, 1977.
- Monaco, R. *The Grail War* New York: Pocket, 1979.
- Monaco, R. *The Final Quest* New York: Putnam, 1980.
- Mosse, K. *Labyrinth* London: Orion, 2005.
- Muschg, A. *Der rote Ritter* Frankfurt-am-Main: Suhrkamp, 1991.
- Nash, J. *The Grail King* New York: Dorchester, 2006.
- Nye, R. *Merlin* London: Hamilton, 1978.
- Padmore, E.S. *The Death of Arthur* London: Jenkins, 1936. [drama]
- Palov, C.M. *The Templar's Quest* London: Joseph, 2011.
- Park, J. *Raiders* New York: Yen, 2010.
- Powell, A. *The Fisher King* London: Norton, 1986.
- Powers, T. *The Drawing of the Dark* New York: Ballantine, 1979.
- Powys, J.C. *A Glastonbury Romance* New York: Simon and Schuster, 1932.
- Reed, M. *One For Sorrow* Scottsdale: Poisoned Pen, 1999.
- Reynolds, A. *Knights of Bretannia* Nottingham: Black Library, 2011.
- Rhys, E. *The Masque of the Grail* London: Matthews, 1908.
- Rickman, P. *The Chalice* London: Macmillan, 1997.
- Robert, D.J. *Kinsmen of the Grail* Boston: Little Brown, 1963.
- Roberts, B. *Sherlock Holmes and the Devil's Grail* London: Constable, 1995.
- Robertson, C. *End of the Century* Amherst: Pyr, 2009.
- Saberhagen, F. *Dominion* New York: Tor, 1982.
- Sapir, R. *Quest* New York: Dutton, 1987.
- Scarrow, A. *The Doomsday Code* New York: Walker, 2012.
- Schwemer, H. *Parzival* Kassel: Barrenreiter, 1948. [drama]

- Sholes, M./Moore, J. *The Grail Conspiracy* Woodbury: Midnight Ink, 2005.
- Shorthouse, J.H. *Sir Percival* London: Macmillan, 1886.
- Southworth, M.E. *Galahad, Knight Errant* Boston: Graham, 1907.
- Spradin, M.P. *Keeper of the Grail* New York: Putnam, 2008.
- Spradin, M.P. *Orphan of Destiny* New York: Putnam, 2010.
- Spradin, M.P. *Trail of Fate* New York: Putnam, 2003.
- Sterling, S. *A Lady at King Arthur's Court* London: Chatto and Windus, 1909.
- Stewart, M. *The Prince and the Pilgrim* London: Coronet, 1999.
- Stone, M. *Alien Sea* London: Hodder, 1998.
- Strauer, V. *Worldstone* New York: Macmillan, 1985.
- Stucken, E. *Der Gral* Berlin: Reiss, 1924.
- Taylor, T.H. *Parsifal* Sydney: Angus and Robertson, 1906. [drama]
- Tennyson, A. *Idylls of the King* (many editions) [poetry]
- Trevor, M. *The Sparrow Child* London: Collins, 1958.
- Tucker, I. StJ. *The Sangreal* Chicago: the author, 1919.
- Underhill, U. *The Column of Dust* London: Methuen, 1909.
- Vance, J. *The Green Road* London: Gollancz, 2003.
- Vance, J. *Lyonesse: Madouc* Novato: Underwood-Miller, 1989.
- Webb, C. *Eusebius the Phoenician* New York: Funk and Wagnalls, 1969.
- White, T.H. *The Once and Future King* London: Collins, 1958.
- Williams, C. *War in Heaven* London: Gollancz, 1920.
- Yamaguchi, M. *Arm of Kannon* Los Angeles: Tokyopop, 2004.
- Yunge-Bateman, E. *The Flowering Thorn* n.p.: the author, 1961.
- Zink, M. *Déodat* Paris: Seuil, 2002.

# APPENDIX TWO

## The Search for the Cauldron

It will be seen from the contents of the work before you that the present writer considers it very likely that the story of the Grail stems from that of a journey leading the protagonists to a place with a sacred cauldron and that this place is the Otherworld. Now the Celts - and the reader is reminded that when I speak of Celts I do so in cultural and linguistic, rather than racial, terms - regarded the Otherworld as a somewhat parallel universe, which was the home of the gods (who in Christian times were transformed into the fairies) and the dead alike. It was the realm of the dead, but not only of the dead.

A number of stories found in Irish MSS. Have parallels with the Grail saga. One such is *Togail Bruidne Da Derga* 'The Destruction of Da Derga's Hostel'. While the earliest extant MS of this dates from the 12<sup>th</sup> Century, the saga, even in written form, is considerably older. And who was this Da Derga, whose dwelling was so destroyed. His name means 'the Red God' and he is almost certainly identical with the Dagda, the chief of the Irish gods. Both had a famous cauldron.

Below, I give a part of this tale:-

There was a king in Ireland named Conaire [3 *syl.*] and when he ruled the country flourished. Crops grew in abundance, the summer sun was rarely hidden by clouds and no wind blew before noon: for a good king rules a prosperous land.

There was a brigand in the country whose name was Ingcel the One-Eyed and, though he had but one eye, it had nine pupils. The king banished this desperado to Britain, where he continued as a freebooter. One day, he determined to return to Ireland, with a great company, to be avenged on King Conaire.

Kings in Ireland were placed under special ritual prohibitions. They broke them at their peril. Alas, Conaire broke a number of his.

As he was riding along one day with his entourage and he asked one of them, *Where shall we bide this night? My friend Da Derga lives nearby. Let us fare to his hostel.*

Now one of the prohibitions placed on Conaire was the somewhat enigmatic *Reds you shall not follow to the house of Red* and in the Irish tongue *dearga* means red. Perhaps this did not occur to Conaire at first. But then they saw ahead of them three riders. Completely clad in red were they and even their hair was red. Three times did Conaire send a messenger to them, telling them to fall to the rear of the King, but each time they refused; and, as to their nature, one of them remarked, *Though we are alive, we are dead. There will be great destruction after nightfall. Swords will be bloodied, crows will feast, ravens gorge themselves.* And they entered the hostel of Da Derga.

Da Derga had built this hostel and in it was a cauldron that never ceased to boil. It supplied food for the nation of the Irish. Its doors were never closed, save on the windward side. Red hair had he and red eyebrows and his cheeks too were reddish of hue. To the servants of the house he would give food and drink for his guests. And he welcomed Conaire when he arrived. His hostel had this peculiarity: the River Dodder ran through it.

Now Ingcel Caoch returned to Ireland and that night he besieged the hostel and set it afire. The fire was put out by the waters of the Dodder. As the fighting continued, a great thirst overwhelmed Conaire. All the water had been used up in quenching the fire, so one of his warriors, MacCecht, betook himself from the building and went in search of water. As the fighting continued, the King expired, not from battle-wounds, but from raging thirst.

A drought had seized Ireland and MacCecht had to look hither and yon before he found water. When he returned, the fight was over and he beheld two warriors cutting off the head of the King. These he slew and into the mouth of the head he poured water. And the head spoke, praising MacCecht, saying that, were it but alive, great indeed would have been MacCecht's reward.

This story shows some relation to the Grail story in that Conaire and his followers journey to the Otherworld (in Ireland these magic hostels, of which there were reputedly five, had Otherworldly locations) where they find a vessel that provides food and drink and there is also an interesting feature in the depiction of a talking head, to which we shall return shortly.

A variant tale is called *Togail Bruidne Da Choca* which is set in the modern county of Westmeath. Here the hostel is the property of Da Choca, but his name too means 'the Red God'. In it the hero Cormac is besieged by the Connachtmen, who set fire to the hostel repeatedly, and eventually Cormac is killed in the affray.

T.F. O'Rahilly has argued with cogency that entry to the house is entry to the realm of the dead. By entering it, both Conaire and Cormac were in fact dying. The Otherworld features both gods and the dead and the Red God presides over it.

In the Grail saga, the heroes are seeking a magic vessel. We have seen, however, that the vessel is probably that sought by Arthur in *Preiddeu Annwn* and *Culhwch ac Olwen* (where the Other-world has been euhemerised into Ireland). In *Branwen,* Bran is not specifically seeking the cauldron in Ireland (=the Otherworld), but it is there. Men thrown into it when dead are revived, but they cannot speak. (The dead do not talk). Bran's head, like Conaire's, is cut off, but speaks afterwards.

In all of this, we see the *motif* of a cauldron, generally of plenty, but also of life and the two elements are not unconnected. A journey to the realm of the dead, which can only be accessed by dying, is perhaps the underlying foundation of the tale. It is a death tale.

However, what about these talking heads. In *Peredur* a disembodied though non-talking head replaces the Grail and the notion of a disembodied head seems to have a firm connection with whatever original form the tale took. The answer may lie in the fact that there was a cult of the head among the Celts and it may be that the heads of dead heroes were regarded as talismanic or oracular. It is possible that heads were buried to protect tribal areas, as we see Bran's head was buried to protect Britain, or preserved for use in giving prophecies (perhaps helped by some ventriloquial druid).

One might ask how such a myth could have been transported to Britain from Ireland. It could be the case that it was originally a basic myth of the Celts and both stories came from an original common source. However, there were also a number of Irish settlements in Britain from the latter days of the Roman Empire, notably in Dyfed where an Irish dynasty ruled, and these may have carried the story across the Irish Sea. The attendance on the cauldron by Nine Maidens seems to be a purely British aspect of the story.

With regard to Da Derga, he is sometimes simply called *Derg* (red) and the name Derg is also given to a god probably identical in origin who is strongly associated with death. He may even have been identical with the god Donn, who was very much a god of death. The hostel of Da Derga is actually referred to as the House of Donn. It would seem that the original Grail Castle was the House of Death. However, the Celts do not seem to have regarded the Otherworldly realm of the dead as threatening. Did not the gods live there too? It was said by the Romans that, so firm was the belief of the Celts in the Otherworld, that they would lend money to be paid back in the next life.

Just when the story of the Cauldron might have become the story of the Grail, if indeed it did, we cannot say. It was presumably brought to Brittany by the Britons who migrated thither in the 6th Century. Perhaps it was Chrétien himself who christianised the story. After all, Chrétien does mean a Christian.

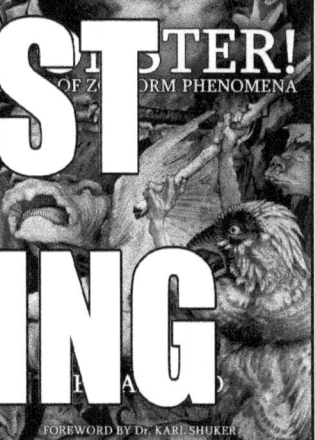

# THE WORLD'S WEIRDEST PUBLISHING COMPANY

# HOW TO START A PUBLISHING EMPIRE

Unlike most mainstream publishers, we have a non-commercial remit, and our mission statement claims that "we publish books because they deserve to be published, not because we think that we can make money out of them". Our motto is the Latin Tag *Pro bona causa facimus* (we do it for good reason), a slogan taken from a children's book *The Case of the Silver Egg* by the late Desmond Skirrow.

WIKIPEDIA: "The first book published was in 1988. *Take this Brother may it Serve you Well* was a guide to Beatles bootlegs by Jonathan Downes. It sold quite well, but was hampered by very poor production values, being photocopied, and held together by a plastic clip binder. In 1988 A5 clip binders were hard to get hold of, so the publishers took A4 binders and cut them in half with a hacksaw. It now reaches surprisingly high prices second hand.

The production quality improved slightly over the years, and after 1999 all the books produced were ringbound with laminated colour covers. In 2004, however, they signed an agreement with Lightning Source, and all books are now produced perfect bound, with full colour covers."

Until 2010 all our books, the majority of which are/were on the subject of mystery animals and allied disciplines, were published by `CFZ Press`, the publishing arm of the Centre for Fortean Zoology (CFZ), and we urged our readers and followers to draw a discreet veil over the books that we published that were completely off topic to the CFZ.

However, in 2010 we decided that enough was enough and launched a second imprint, `Fortean Words` which aims to cover a wide range of non animal-related esoteric subjects. Other imprints will be launched as and when we feel like it, however the basic ethos of the company remains the same: Our job is to publish books and magazines that we feel are worth publishing, whether or not they are going to sell. Money is, after all - as my dear old Mama once told me - a rather vulgar subject, and she would be rolling in her grave if she thought that her eldest son was somehow in `trade`.

Luckily, so far our tastes have turned out not to be that rarified after all, and we have sold far more books than anyone ever thought that we would, so there is a moral in there somewhere...

Jon Downes,
Woolsery, North Devon
July 2010

# CFZ PRESS

## Other Books in Print

*ORANG PENDEK: Sumatra's Forgotten Ape* by Richard Freeman
*THE MYSTERY ANIMALS OF THE BRITISH ISLES: London* by Neil Arnold
*CFZ EXPEDITION REPORT: India 2010* by Richard Freeman *et al*
*The Cryptid Creatures of Florida* by Scott Marlow
*Dead of Night* by Lee Walker
*The Mystery Animals of the British Isles: The Northern Isles* by Glen Vaudrey
*THE MYSTERY ANIMALS OF THE BRTISH ISLES: Gloucestershire and Worcestershire* by
Paul Williams
*When Bigfoot Attacks* by Michael Newton
*Weird Waters – The Mystery Animals of Scandinavia: Lake and Sea Monsters* by Lars Thomas
*The Inhumanoids* by Barton Nunnelly
*Monstrum! A Wizard's Tale* by Tony "Doc" Shiels
*CFZ Yearbook 2011* edited by Jonathan Downes
*Karl Shuker's Alien Zoo* by Shuker, Dr Karl P.N
*Tetrapod Zoology Book One* by Naish, Dr Darren
*The Mystery Animals of Ireland* by Gary Cunningham and Ronan Coghlan
*Monsters of Texas* by Gerhard, Ken
*The Great Yokai Encyclopaedia* by Freeman, Richard
*NEW HORIZONS: Animals & Men issues 16-20 Collected Editions Vol. 4*
by Downes, Jonathan
*A Daintree Diary -*
*Tales from Travels to the Daintree Rainforest in tropical north Queensland, Australia*
by Portman, Carl
*Strangely Strange but Oddly Normal* by Roberts, Andy
*Centre for Fortean Zoology Yearbook 2010* by Downes, Jonathan
*Predator Deathmatch* by Molloy, Nick
*Star Steeds and other Dreams* by Shuker, Karl
*CHINA: A Yellow Peril?* by Muirhead, Richard
*Mystery Animals of the British Isles: The Western Isles* by Vaudrey, Glen

*Giant Snakes - Unravelling the coils of mystery* by Newton, Michael
*Mystery Animals of the British Isles: Kent* by Arnold, Neil
*Centre for Fortean Zoology Yearbook 2009* by Downes, Jonathan
*CFZ EXPEDITION REPORT: Russia 2008* by Richard Freeman *et al*, Shuker, Karl (fwd)
*Dinosaurs and other Prehistoric Animals on Stamps - A Worldwide catalogue*
by Shuker, Karl P. N
*Dr Shuker's Casebook* by Shuker, Karl P.N
*The Island of Paradise - chupacabra UFO crash retrievals,*
*and accelerated evolution on the island of Puerto Rico* by Downes, Jonathan
*The Mystery Animals of the British Isles: Northumberland and Tyneside* by Hallowell, Michael J
*Centre for Fortean Zoology Yearbook 1997* by Downes, Jonathan (Ed)
*Centre for Fortean Zoology Yearbook 2002* by Downes, Jonathan (Ed)
*Centre for Fortean Zoology Yearbook 2000/1* by Downes, Jonathan (Ed)
*Centre for Fortean Zoology Yearbook 1998* by Downes, Jonathan (Ed)
*Centre for Fortean Zoology Yearbook 2003* by Downes, Jonathan (Ed)
*In the wake of Bernard Heuvelmans* by Woodley, Michael A
*CFZ EXPEDITION REPORT: Guyana 2007* by Richard Freeman *et al*, Shuker, Karl (fwd)
*Centre for Fortean Zoology Yearbook 1999* by Downes, Jonathan (Ed)
*Big Cats in Britain Yearbook 2008* by Fraser, Mark (Ed)
*Centre for Fortean Zoology Yearbook 1996* by Downes, Jonathan (Ed)
*THE CALL OF THE WILD - Animals & Men issues 11-15*
*Collected Editions Vol. 3* by Downes, Jonathan (ed)
*Ethna's Journal* by Downes, C N
*Centre for Fortean Zoology Yearbook 2008* by Downes, J (Ed)
*DARK DORSET -Calendar Custome* by Newland, Robert J
*Extraordinary Animals Revisited* by Shuker, Karl
*MAN-MONKEY - In Search of the British Bigfoot* by Redfern, Nick
*Dark Dorset Tales of Mystery, Wonder and Terror* by Newland, Robert J and Mark North
*Big Cats Loose in Britain* by Matthews, Marcus
*MONSTER! - The A-Z of Zooform Phenomena* by Arnold, Neil
*The Centre for Fortean Zoology 2004 Yearbook* by Downes, Jonathan (Ed)
*The Centre for Fortean Zoology 2007 Yearbook* by Downes, Jonathan (Ed)
*CAT FLAPS! Northern Mystery Cats* by Roberts, Andy
*Big Cats in Britain Yearbook 2007* by Fraser, Mark (Ed)
*BIG BIRD! - Modern sightings of Flying Monsters* by Gerhard, Ken
*THE NUMBER OF THE BEAST - Animals & Men issues 6-10*
*Collected Editions Vol. 1* by Downes, Jonathan (Ed)
*IN THE BEGINNING - Animals & Men issues 1-5 Collected Editions Vol. 1* by Downes, Jonathan
*STRENGTH THROUGH KOI - They saved Hitler's Koi and other stories*
by Downes, Jonathan
*The Smaller Mystery Carnivores of the Westcountry* by Downes, Jonathan
*CFZ EXPEDITION REPORT: Gambia 2006* by Richard Freeman *et al*, Shuker, Karl (fwd)
*The Owlman and Others* by Jonathan Downes
*The Blackdown Mystery* by Downes, Jonathan

*Big Cats in Britain Yearbook 2006* by Fraser, Mark (Ed)
*Fragrant Harbours - Distant Rivers* by Downes, John T
*Only Fools and Goatsuckers* by Downes, Jonathan
*Monster of the Mere* by Jonathan Downes
*Dragons:More than a Myth* by Freeman, Richard Alan
*Granfer's Bible Stories* by Downes, John Tweddell
*Monster Hunter* by Downes, Jonathan

# Fortean Words

The Centre for Fortean Zoology has for several years led the field in Fortean publishing. CFZ Press is the only publishing company specialising in books on monsters and mystery animals. CFZ Press has published more books on this subject than any other company in history and has attracted such well known authors as Andy Roberts, Nick Redfern, Michael Newton, Dr Karl Shuker, Neil Arnold, Dr Darren Naish, Jon Downes, Ken Gerhard and Richard Freeman.

Now CFZ Press are launching a new imprint. Fortean Words is a new line of books dealing with Fortean subjects other than cryptozoology, which is - after all - the subject the CFZ are best known for. Fortean Words is being launched with a spectacular multi-volume series called *Haunted Skies* which covers British UFO sightings between 1940 and 2010. Former policeman John Hanson and his long-suffering partner Dawn Holloway have compiled a peerless library of sighting reports, many that have not been made public before.

Other books include a look at the Berwyn Mountains UFO case by renowned Fortean Andy Roberts and a series of forthcoming books by transatlantic researcher Nick Redfern. CFZ Press are dedicated to maintaining the fine quality of their works with Fortean Words. New authors tackling new subjects will always be encouraged, and we hope that our books will continue to be as ground-breaking and popular as ever.

*Haunted Skies Volume One 1940-1959* by John Hanson and Dawn Holloway
*Haunted Skies Volume Two 1960-1965* by John Hanson and Dawn Holloway
*Haunted Skies Volume Three 1965-1967* by John Hanson and Dawn Holloway
*Haunted Skies Volume Four 1968-1971* by John Hanson and Dawn Holloway
*Grave Concerns* by Kai Roberts

*Police and the Paranormal* by Andy Owens
*Dead of Night* by Lee Walker
*Space Girl Dead on Spaghetti Junction* - an anthology by Nick Redfern
*I Fort the Lore* - an anthology by Paul Screeton
*UFO Down - the Berwyn Mountains UFO Crash* by Andy Roberts

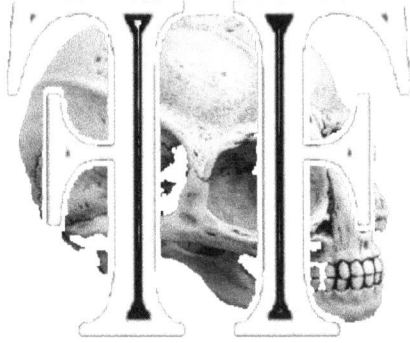

# Fortean Fiction

J ust before Christmas 2011, we launched our third imprint, this time dedicated to - let's see if you guessed it from the title - fictional books with a Fortean or cryptozoological theme. We have published a few fictional books in the past, but now think that because of our rising reputation as publishers of quality Forteana, that a dedicated fiction imprint was the order of the day.

We launched with four titles:

*Green Unpleasant Land* by Richard Freeman
*Left Behind* by Harriet Wadham
*Dark Ness* by Tabitca Cope
*Snap!* By Steven Bredice